Staying Put
in Lane County

Whitey Lueck

I wish to extend my gratitude to
Andrea Heid—who was my assiduous proofreader—and
Helen Liu, who designed the book's cover.

Cover photo: Oregon oxalis and Pacific swordfern carpet the forest floor at an elevation of 1,800 feet in the Cascades Mountains of eastern Lane County. (Photo taken by the author.)

"I read one or two shallow books of travel in the intervals of my work,
till that employment made me ashamed of myself,
and I asked where it was that I lived."

Henry David Thoreau, in *Walden*

CONTENTS

Preface ix

January First: Day Number One 1

A Case of Mistaken Identify 4

The No-Smoking Car 7

Finding Rose 10

Ravens, Nuthatches, and Aircraft 13

Unwanted Abbreviations 15

Leaving the Fog Behind 17

Whitey's World and How It Works 19

Things with Wings 27

Balm of Gilead 29

A Four-Course Breakfast in a Five-Star Restaurant 32

An Aromatic Little Forest Denizen 34

White-Flower Week 36

A Visit to Tire Mountain 38

Nature Rolls Out the Pink Carpet for Me 43

After the Dawn Chorus 45

A Story of Two Towheads 48

A Midsummer's Morn 51

Lane County's Northwest Corner 53

Lane Country's Southwest Corner 57

My Ascent of El Popo 62

Lane County's Two Summertime Faces 65

Fruits du Jour—and a Vegetable 68

Two Common Misconceptions 71

The Intruder 74

Aufderheide Drive: A Dream Come True 77

An Interrupted Nap 82

Celebration 84

Lane County's Southeast Corner 87

Lane County's Northeast Corner 91

One Thousand Days 94

The Noisiest Border Crossing 97

Prescient Parents 102

White-Fronted Geese 105

Sounds of the Fourth Day of Fall 107

Lane County's *Other* Three Sisters 109

A Landscape Shaped by Fire and Ice 114

Sitting on a Defunct Railroad 118

Why I Hate Cars 122

The Incredible Shrinking Lane County 129

Josh's Remark 131

An Apparently Common Misrepresentation of Lane County 134

Habitat Loss—and Habitat Gain 136

A Change of Air, A Change of Attitude 139

The Wind That Wasn't 141

Stevie's Question 143

The Bench 146

Christmas Eve at the Border 150

A Troubling Peek at Our Corrections System 155

Don't Fence Me Out 161

A Message from Jesus 165

Rose 168

December Thirty-First 174

PREFACE

After spending 460 consecutive days within the borders of Lane County, I knowingly slipped across the border yesterday into Lincoln County for a couple of hours. I'd decided to take part in a one-day field trip to the central Oregon coast with the Eugene Natural History Society, part of which included a brief lecture atop Cape Perpetua. As we passed the sign, "Welcome to Lincoln County—Heart of the Oregon Coast," no alarms went off. No marching bands played. I was neither elated by the event nor disappointed in myself. It just happened.

After a lunch of fish-and-chips at Leroy's Blue Whale restaurant in Yachats and the talk at Cape Perpetua, our group returned to Lane County to spend the afternoon visiting the Audubon Society's Ten Mile Creek Sanctuary, about five miles inland from the Pacific. The field trip ended, then, late afternoon with a brief visit to lower Ten Mile Creek, where a rotary screw trap—a large, floating metal apparatus which funnels fish into a live box, from which the fish can be removed and examined—is operated by the Oregon Department of Fish and Wildlife. There, we observed the trap's harvest for the day: dozens of tiny fall chinook salmon fry, just a month or two old; coho salmon smolts, a year or two old and now heading for the ocean; and a five-inch-long baby Pacific lamprey.

When it was time for the rest of the group to turn south on Highway 101 and head back to Eugene, the car I was riding in turned north, instead, and drove me to just past Bob Creek, where I got out of the car in a light rain, shouldered my red Kelty backpack, bid farewell to my trip-mates, and quickly and quietly disappeared into the woods behind a curtain of head-high swordferns. I'd finally returned to *Te Moana Nui A Kiwa*—my coastal sanctuary since the early 2000s—after an absence of exactly four years.

Back in the mid-2000s, I was visiting this area three or four times a year, alone, to spend a few days each time in two of the most awe-inspiring landscapes that Lane County and the planet have to offer. Right at the edge of the Pacific is a stretch of Oregon's spectacular "high coast" of rocky headlands—from Cape Perpetua to Heceta Head—that are separated by sandy beaches, secluded coves, and coastal bluffs topped by either grassland or spruce forest. And just a little bit inland, in the protected coastal valleys from Gwynn Creek in the north to Cape Creek at Heceta Head, are some of the finest remaining examples of temperate rainforests, with towering Sitka spruces festooned with clumps of epiphytic leather-leaf ferns the size of laundry baskets, and bigleaf maples simply smothered with mosses and licorice ferns. All of these plants thrive in the central coast's year-round moist and mild climate where it rains in the winter and there is almost daily ocean fog in the summer, and year-round temperatures seldom go below freezing or above 75 degrees.

That climate suits me just fine, as well, and is the principal reason I chose this area as one of my two "second homes"—along with the West Cascades near McKenzie Bridge. Unlike the McKenzie Valley, however, this part of Oregon's coast is not served by public transit. But I am blessed to know several Eugeneans who come to the central coast on a regular basis. Two of them have second homes here—*real* houses, that is, not just a verdant glade in the woods that's barely big enough for a tent. And a third goes to a pet-friendly motel in Yachats at the end of most every term at the university, to focus on grading her students' finals and, when she needs to take a break, she can spend a little quiet time with her dog on the nearby beach. Thanks to these generous people, I can come to the coast almost any time I like, even though I don't own a car.

As the brief shower was letting up after my short hike through the spruce woods, I set up my tent right here in the mossy middle of the old coast "highway," one of very few flat spots that has neither trees nor ferns growing on it. Before the paved Roosevelt Coast Military Highway—later renamed simply the Oregon Coast Highway—was completed in 1932, residents and visitors traveled along a dirt road carved into the then-grassy hillsides along the "high coast," and then sped across the sand just above the waterline along sections of "low coast" such as the dune-dominated areas both north and south of Florence.

Over the years, I've discovered along this part of the coast quite a few pieces of the old road that are still very visible and walkable. Other sections have become completely overgrown, or been replaced by the new highway, or they've fallen off into the ocean where the road followed the edge of a coastal terrace or bluff. In fact, having been away from this bluff-top spot for four years, I considered the possibility that it, too, had in the interim been swallowed by the sea. But it's still here.

I first came across the name I've given my coastal sanctuary—*Te Moana Nui A Kiwa* (tay moh-AH-nah NOO-ee ah kee-WAH)—several decades ago in a book about the South Pacific by James Norman Hall and Charles Nordhoff, authors of the famous *Mutiny on the Bounty* trilogy along with many other books about the area. It's a Maori phrase and is said to mean The Great Sea of Kiwa, which is how the Maori people (of present-day New Zealand) once referred to the Pacific Ocean. I do not by any means dislike the name, Pacific Ocean, but I found the Polynesian name to be so poetic that I attached it to this spot of which I'm so very fond.

It's fitting that I've come here to write the Preface to this collection of essays about my year in Lane County—as well as to have a few days of peace-and-quiet at the edge of the North American continent. First, I've written many essays over the past decade or so right here. And second, from the front door of my tent, I can see Captain Cook Ridge, which dives into the ocean at Captain Cook Point, Lane County's northwest corner. In mid-2014, I wrote one of the essays in this collection at that very point.

With only one or two exceptions, the essays here were written during my days (and sometimes nights) in the woods—mostly in the West Cascades—where I spend much of my time. My days alone in the woods are what I call "reflection time" for me, when my mind is clearest and when I have virtually no distractions. In a perhaps shocking departure from the contemporary norm, all of the essays began with pencil drafts, and many of them were written by candlelight inside my tent. Although I do use computers, I don't own one. I prefer, instead, to keep computers at "arm's length" by writing an essay's first draft longhand, and digitizing it later on the library computers at the University of Oregon. I do not edit my essays at the computer, but go through two or more printed versions of the essay before it's considered finished.

At the beginning of 2014, I didn't yet know what kinds of essays I'd be writing for this book. Yes, I knew I wanted to do at least a few on the geography of Lane County, and of some favorite places of mine that others might enjoy reading about. And two of the essays were inspired by my students, who wanted to know more about my "lifestyle" and why I had such strong opinions about privately-owned automobiles.

What about the rest? Initially, I thought all of the essays should be about Lane County itself. But even though I never physically left the county during 2014, my mind wandered more than a few times beyond the county's borders to other places I lived in my younger years. So there are several essays about events that occurred during my so-called peripatetic years in the 1970s and early 1980s when I lived and worked part of the time in western Europe and traveled fairly extensively. I thought that because those "mental wanderings" were part of my year in Lane County, I was justified in including them here. And those essays might of course provide additional insights about some of the events in my earlier life that contributed to the person—and the writer—I am today.

I knew from the outset, however, that I didn't want the essays to be just a "travelogue" about Lane County. Sure, I might introduce readers to a place or two they could be unfamiliar with—or to a particular aspect of a place they thought they knew well, but about which I have a somewhat different perspective. But I also wanted the essays to be snapshots of my own life during the course of the year—what kinds of things happened to one particular individual, me, and some of the thoughts that coursed through my head during a single calendar year. So this collection of essays also includes, for example, reflections about some of my personal celebrations and anniversaries, as well as the passing of a dear friend.

The essays provide glimpses, too, of some of the natural phenomena that make Lane County—like any other county—unique. They include bird migrations, flowering times for different plants, the "soundscapes" of different locations, and creatures native to Lane County that readers may not be familiar with. Although most of the essays can be said to be about "nature"—since I spend so much time out of doors and out of town, I'm happy to say—a fair percentage also address urban and sometimes personal issues that, I'm hopeful, will also be of interest to readers. In short, there should be something for everyone in this little compilation. There are likely several essays that will make you laugh—or at least smile—and one or two that could even make you shed a tear or two. And the reader is sure to react to some essays by saying, "I didn't know that!" or "I never thought about that before!"

But most of all, I hope that whosoever peruses these pages enjoys *reading* about the 365-day-long journey that was "my year in Lane County" as much as I enjoyed *living* the year that is portrayed here.

Whitey Lueck
Te Moana Nui A Kiwa
Tuesday, 24 March 2015

JANUARY FIRST: DAY NUMBER ONE

Actually, it's Day Number Sixteen already, but who's counting? Well, *I'm* counting.

When I decided to purposely remain within the boundaries of Lane County for an entire year, I chose a *calendar* year—from January 1 through December 31. But in fact, the last time I set foot outside of Lane County was sixteen days ago. I took the train from Eugene to Salem, then visited friends in both Aurora and Portland before returning to Eugene on December 16, 2013.

Today, however, was the first day of my *calendar* year in Lane County. I didn't have any special plans for it, just as I don't yet have any particular plans about the essays I hope to write during the course of the coming year. I'll just see what develops.

Accordingly, I left my house just after dawn this morning and bicycled to the Market-of-Choice grocery a few blocks away. My preferred time of day to visit the store is early morning, soon after it opens at seven o'clock. At that time, there is still very little traffic on the streets; I enjoy seeing the morning sky; and I avoid running into too many acquaintances at the grocery, other than my favorite checkout clerk or two. Call me antisocial, but when I go to the grocery, I go with the idea of accomplishing that errand as quickly and efficiently as possible, so I can move on to the rest of my day.

But this morning, when I came back outside and was distributing my purchases between my two bike baskets, who should walk up to me but a friend I hadn't seen in several years. Now retired and a bit reclusive himself in some ways, it's no surprise that his path seldom intersects mine, even though we live in the same ZIP code. He's a retired language professor of some renown internationally, and we first met perhaps ten years ago, when he hired me to advise him about the health of the trees on his property in Eugene's south hills. He's also the father of one of my good friends.

We had a nice chat there by the bike rack and of course I just had to tell him—the first personal friend I'd seen today—that this was Day Number One of the year during which I would not leave Lane County. He looked at me and said, "Whitey, I haven't left Lane County in [brief pause while he did the math] seventeen years." He didn't say this in a dismissive way at all, but just matter-of-factly. I didn't know what to say, but I *did* feel as if he'd stolen a bit of my thunder, even if he didn't mean to.

After a few more seconds, he added, "Oh, come to think of it, I went to Veneta a couple of times to the Oregon Country Fair." I laughed, and informed my dear friend—who grew up in another country and missed out on learning about Oregon's geography in grade school—that Veneta, only fifteen miles west of Eugene, was still in Lane County. And then he laughed, too.

At one point in his life, my friend had traveled all over the world, mostly to attend professional conferences where he presented papers he'd written in his field of expertise. But by the time he'd reached his late 50s, he'd tired of that routine and elected to settle down in Eugene, with no particular desire to ever leave again. He's able to meet almost all of his needs by going no farther than a mile or two from his house.

How about that? Here I am, thinking I'm doing something unusual—or maybe even difficult—by staying in the county for an entire calendar year, and on Day Number One I run into someone who hasn't left in nearly two decades, and doesn't find that fact particularly noteworthy! The difference between the two of us, of course, is that my own "confinement" is a very purposeful one: I intend to stay here in Lane County and write a series of essays about my year. If I hadn't made this decision, my life—especially because of my OUT-OF-DOORS business where I teach field classes throughout the West—likely would have taken me a few other places during 2014, at least elsewhere in western Oregon, if not to other places on the West Coast, such as western Washington or northern California.

But my friend's decision seventeen or so years ago to no longer attend professional conferences or travel for any other reason, was simply because he'd tired of that life and was looking forward to staying home for a while.

He didn't see his decision at that time as particularly restrictive or confining, nor did he discount the possibility of leaving Eugene again sometime in the future. It just so happened that one year in Eugene led to the next, and now it's added up to seventeen years already.

In my case, I'm truly looking forward to staying in Lane County the entire year, and I don't think I'll have to exercise too much restraint in sticking to my plan.

A CASE OF MISTAKEN IDENTITY

I had stopped briefly at the edge of the narrow forest road just to listen to the quiet when, about 75 yards ahead, I saw a dark brown animal with short legs making its way across the road. The animal had just exited a recently thinned stand of young trees on the left, and was headed toward a stand of centuries-old Douglas-firs on the right. I saw it for only a few seconds before it disappeared into the low vegetation on the right side of the road.

I was still standing at the roadside and pondering what kind of animal I could have seen, when, to my astonishment, it went back across the road and re-entered the stand of fifty-year-old trees. So I got a second look at it. It was clearly a mustelid of some sort—small carnivores such as weasels, otters, and wolverines. But which one?

I am familiar with most of the mustelids native to Oregon's Cascade Mountains, having seen before mink, river otter, both weasels (short-tailed and long-tailed), and pine marten. And I knew which mustelids it could *not* be. It was too big, for example, for a weasel; and probably too low in elevation for a marten. I decided that it had to have been either a mink or a river otter.

However, when I'd previously seen a mink or an otter, the animal was either in the water or very near it. This animal was at least 50 feet from a tiny creek that flowed among the old trees to the right side of the road, yet it simply *had* to be one of the two, as there were no other mustelids that one might be likely to see at the 1,800-foot elevation in the West Cascades and abroad in the daytime.

Some of the distinctive characteristics of the animal were its relatively high rear haunches as it made its way across the road; its dark brown, almost black color; its size—some three feet long, from the tip of its nose to the end of its tail; and its bushy, blunt-tipped tail over a foot in length.

The river otters I'd seen in the past had stout, densely hairy tails that ended in a point, and were not bushy or fluffy like this animal's tail. Plus, I recall otters hopping or "galloping" in a bouncy way when moving on land, and this animal moved more linearly.

That left mink. This animal, however, was really too big for a mink, but what else *could* it be? After a minute or two, I proceeded up the road to the point where the animal had entered the thinned stand. I stood still for a bit, thinking I might catch another glimpse of it, but saw nothing. Perhaps the animal, alerted to my presence by then, was keeping a low profile and not moving, to escape detection. So I continued on up the ridge, where I spent the remainder of the day. I was excited to have seen a mink for the first time in years, but I thought little more about the sighting, except to write about it in my journal later that day.

Several weeks later, while riding the bus back to town after another day spent in the same area, I had a conversation with one of the National Forest's wildlife biologists—also riding the same bus home after her workday at the ranger station—and we were discussing various research projects going on in the National Forest to determine the presence or absence of carnivores such as lynx and wolverine, which are extremely rare in Oregon. I mentioned to her that I'd seen a mink several weeks before, which she found interesting, as she'd seen them before, too, but only in Canada.

As our conversation continued, she mentioned "trail cameras" that have been installed at high elevations in the Cascades in an effort to possibly photograph a lynx or wolverine. But she also mentioned that in the ranger district just south of the one where she works—and where I spend so much time—someone recently discovered the image of a Pacific fisher when analyzing trail-cam footage. My eyes lit up. Pacific fisher? I didn't even know that they were found in Oregon.

By that time, we had arrived at her bus stop and she stepped off without me saying anything more. But the rest of the way back to town, and later that evening at my desk, I ruminated on those two words that had so rattled me back in the bus: Pacific fisher. Of course! When I looked again at my sketches and reconsidered how I came up with mink in the first place—

"Mink or otter? Definitely not otter, so . . . mink!"—I realized the mistake I'd made, based simply on my lack of knowledge that the fisher is indeed occasionally seen in our area.

The following week, I conferred briefly with another wildlife biologist at the ranger station about my sighting, which by then I was very confident of. And he quizzed me about other possibilities such as pine marten, but I stood by my assertion that I'd actually seen a Pacific fisher—for the reasons mentioned above—and shortly thereafter filed a report on my sighting for the ranger station.

Looking back now on how I'd made my first decision about the animal I'd seen—then later changed it—I was reminded that all of us do this in a variety of settings. My students who learn just three species of pines in my Trees Across Oregon course then attempt to identify *any* pine they come across as one of those three, when there are in fact more than a dozen species of pines planted in our area. In an effort to help them avoid misidentifying a pine species they may not have encountered before, I encourage them to say to themselves: I know only three species of pine—is this tree in fact one of those species, or is it a species I'm not yet familiar with?

I need to practice what I preach a little bit more. The animal that I saw was much too big for a mink, and yet I convinced myself, based on the limited information I had, that that's what it simply *had* to be.

It's still a little hard for me to grasp that on the second day of January this year I in fact saw a Pacific fisher—probably a once-in-a-lifetime sighting for me. And I have to smile when I recall the thought process I went through to (mis)identify the animal as a mink, and then, because I had seen mink before, I thought little more of the animal. That is, until someone mentioned the presence of another related but very rare animal that is occasionally seen in the area, an animal that I had never even considered.

THE NO-SMOKING CAR

During my multi-year residence in Western Europe in the 1970s, one of my favorite activities was riding the trains. I was enthralled by the beautiful and varied landscapes that train travel exposed me to—from the vineyard-covered rolling hills of western France, to the jagged, snow-covered Alps of Switzerland and the bright yellow rape-seed fields of pancake-flat southern Sweden.

But just as fascinating were the beautiful and varied *people* traveling with me. Sometimes, in a single train compartment, the passengers came from several different countries. Western European countries were the best represented, to be sure, but I recall meeting South Africans, New Zealanders, and Brazilians as well.

In order to strike up a conversation, I might ask one of my compartment-mates what crop was growing in a field we were passing, or the name of a distant mountain peak. Although some of my fellow travelers likely understood at least a little English, I usually tried one of my other languages first—French, Swedish, or German, depending on where I was—and didn't let on that I was American.

Sometimes, in an effort to include everyone in the compartment in the conversation, it required a complex series of translations. I'd ask my question in French of a Swiss woman from Geneva, who would in turn translate it to Swiss-German (which I couldn't understand) for her male compatriot from Zürich, and then he—who also knew a little Italian—would tell the fellow from Milan what I'd said or asked. The response of

7

the man from Milan, of course, would be passed back to me in reverse order, accompanied more often than not by smiles all around.

Even if my seatmate learned that I was American, I preferred to speak a language that the two of us knew in common rather than have him possibly struggle to speak English. I thought it fairer for the two of us to each struggle a little—speaking a language that was foreign to both of us— instead of one of us having a language advantage.

One spring, as I was traveling through the western part of what was then West Germany, I was alone in my compartment until a young German man about my age joined me. Within a short while, of course, I'd engaged him in conversation. I probably tried German at first, but we soon switched to French, where we had approximately equal fluency.

When the train stopped near the big U.S. military base at Kaiserslautern, three of my fellow Americans, evidently soldiers on leave, joined my German conversant and me. While Peter and I continued our conversation in French, the newly arrived passengers in our no-smoking car carried on a lively banter in American English that was peppered with profanity.

Soon, one of the young men pulled a pack of cigarettes out of his shirt pocket, and began tapping the bottom of the pack in evident anticipation of having a cigarette. When I noticed this, I said to Peter that I would briefly change from speaking French with him to speaking English with the American preparing to have a smoke, and then I'd quickly return to our conversation in French. And I wanted him to calmly pick up where we'd left off, as if nothing had happened.

Peter agreed and, a few moments later, just after the soldier had at last pulled a cigarette out of the pack and was getting ready to light it, I turned away from Peter and, in my very best American English that I knew the fellow would understand, said to him: "Pardon me, you son-of-a-bitch, but this is a no-smoking car, and if you light that fucking cigarette, no shit, I'll see to it that your ass is tossed off this train so goddam fast, you won't know what happened."

Then I turned back to Peter—who had no idea what I'd just said—and made an effort to resume our conversation. But I was so excited by what I'd just done that it was extremely difficult for me to pretend as if nothing had happened. The three young GIs, meanwhile, were no longer speaking with one another, but instead sat dumbfounded and slack-jawed and just looked at me, and the fellow with the unlit cigarette held it motionless between his thumb and forefinger.

Soon it was time for Peter—a student at the university in Saarbrücken—to get off, and we exchanged addresses, wished each other the best, and shook hands goodbye. The train started up again, and there I was alone in the compartment with the GIs, all three of them still looking a bit stunned. Finally, the one with the cigarette—which by then he'd put back into the pack in his shirt pocket—looked over at me and said, "So where'd you learn to speak English?" "*In the U.S.,*" I said, "*where I grew up.*"

He didn't believe me. After more than a year and a half in Europe, during which time I seldom spoke my native language, my English had acquired a bit of an accent, so I can somewhat understand his disbelief. When he asked me where I'd grown up, I said Pennsylvania. Then began a series of questions to determine the veracity of my claim. "Okay, what's the name of the town that's famous for its chocolate?" My family lived just a half-hour from Hershey, so I luckily knew that answer. "What's the name of New York's baseball team?" Never a fan of sports, I nonetheless had heard of the Yankees, so I got that one right, too.

After a couple of more questions, he acceded that I was in fact American, and the conversation shifted amiably to where *he* was from. "Fort Atkinson, Wisconsin." "*Really? I have relatives there!*" "What're their names?" "*The two who are about your age are Steve and Doug Larson.*" "Oh my god, we went to school together!" "*No kidding!*"

By the time we reached the GIs' stop, I'd exchanged addresses with the young man from "The Fort" and we agreed that, whoever saw the Larsons again first, would have this great story to tell. I don't recall what eventually happened, but that train ride has forever remained a memorable one for me. As someone who never really knew how to swear, nor would have wanted to, it was one of my proudest moments.

FINDING ROSE

I received one day a brief e-mail from Karen—a retired professor whom I know, but don't see even once a year—inquiring whether I knew an elderly woman named Rose and, if so, whether she was still living. My response was immediate: yes, and yes! Rose was very much alive; I had just had coffee with her the day before.

Karen, a hospice volunteer, had been visiting regularly with a terminally ill elderly woman named Iris, who spoke frequently of the fond memories she had of her long-time friend, Rose. But Rose and Iris had drifted apart a decade or so ago, and Iris wanted to contact Rose again, before she succumbed from her illness. Iris especially wanted to apologize for a remark her husband had once made to Rose.

I inquired of Karen how she had connected *me* with Rose. It turned out that she and Iris had looked up Rose's name in the phone book and, finding nothing, they thought Rose might no longer be living. Then Karen did what any good Internet user does these days: a Google search for Rose's name. The solitary item that came up was an article about ginkgo trees that I'd written for the Eugene Tree Foundation's quarterly newsletter in fall 2009. The article included a photo of Rose and me standing by the two ginkgos that grow at the site of a restaurant Rose and her husband once owned. So Karen thought I might by chance know something about Rose.

Karen relayed my message about Rose to Iris, who wanted to telephone Rose, but didn't have Rose's current telephone number. So Karen e-mailed me again, asking if I thought it would be okay for Iris to phone Rose, and if I could provide Rose's number for them. I explained that Rose had trouble hearing, especially on the telephone, so it would be best if Iris wrote Rose a note. And I agreed to hand-deliver the note to Rose, so I could explain how it was that I was involved as an emissary in all of this, and also prepare Rose a little bit for what the note contained and be with her while and after she read the note.

A couple of days later, I received in the mail a letter addressed to Rose, c/o Whitey. As soon as I had the chance, I called Rose to ask if I could stop over. After I'd finished my coffee at her kitchen table, I pulled out the envelope and explained to Rose that I had agreed to deliver to her in person a note from an old friend of hers.

Rose recognized right away the name and return address of the sender— she and Iris had been the very best of friends for many, many years. Rose read the letter to herself. Then she passed it across the table for me to read. It was short and sweet, explaining simply that Iris had always cherished Rose's friendship, and wanted to apologize for causing a rift in that friendship—for an unspecified reason—and would always remember Rose as one of the finest friends a person could ever wish to have.

Rose and I discussed how the two friends had "grown apart," and Rose recalled that Iris's husband had in fact made a comment that Rose found offensive—a xenophobic comment not aimed directly at Rose, but as an immigrant herself (from China), she found his remark insensitive. But that wasn't really why Rose stopped seeing Iris. Rather, Rose said, Iris had become increasingly involved in religious activities that didn't interest Rose, and the two women no longer conversed as comfortably around each other as they once had, as Rose simply wasn't interested in Iris's experiences related to her religion.

I discussed Rose's comments by phone with Karen, who was surprised to learn of this little wrinkle in the story, but agreed that it wasn't worth bringing it up with Iris. Interestingly, both Iris and Rose recalled the remark that Iris's husband had made. From Iris's point of view, that one remark was the cause of the rift in her friendship with Rose; but for Rose, her relationship with Iris had dissolved for an altogether different reason.

Meanwhile, Rose discussed with me what the most suitable response to Iris's note would be. Initially, she wanted to get right in her car and drive over to Iris's house—where Iris lay bedridden—and say hello and goodbye to her old friend, of whom she had such fond memories, despite the years they had been apart.

On second thought, she decided that she preferred to remember Iris as she had been when she was still healthy—not as she might look on her death-bed. So we agreed that writing a note back to Iris would be the best solution. Even though Rose's native language is not English, her written English is elegant and polished, so I knew that she would do a good job.

The next day, Rose appeared at my door, and after I asked her inside, she opened her purse and took out a still-unsealed envelope in which there was a card and a note. She wanted to know if I thought the card was appropriate, and if the sentiments expressed in her note were grammatically correct. As expected, both the card and the note were just perfect for the occasion. So Rose hurried off to the post office without further delay.

Rose's note to Iris was similar to Iris's note to Rose, in that it focused on the wonderful times they'd had together. She acknowledged that the two friends had drifted apart, but assured Iris that she still held her in highest esteem.

Rose and I decided that it was best to send her letter to Iris to *Karen's* address, and let Karen deliver it to Iris, just as I'd done with Iris's letter to Rose. Two days later, Karen phoned me to say that she'd excitedly delivered Rose's letter and that Iris was simply overjoyed to receive it, and was now so very glad she had written a note to Rose in the first place.

Karen and I mused over our critical roles as emissaries and letter-carriers in this touching end-of-life dialogue. We felt blessed to have been able to do what we could to bring these two long-time friends back together again, if only to exchange a few last words that confirmed their mutual admiration for each other.

[To protect the privacy of both the hospice patient and hospice volunteer, their names have been changed in the preceding essay.]

RAVENS, NUTHATCHES, AND AIRCRAFT
Aural Snapshot No. 22

It's early afternoon on 24 February 2014 here at an elevation of 2,000 feet in the West Cascades. After a night of steady but light rain, the skies are clearing and the temperature is an unseasonably mild 55 degrees Fahrenheit. Time once again to examine the area's "soundscape." I do that by recording on paper the different sounds I hear each minute during the course of a single hour—whether the sound occurs just once during the minute, is repetitive, or is constant.

And here are the results; that is, during how many of the 60 minutes each sound was heard at least once:

34 minutes	aircraft
26 minutes	raven
22 minutes	red-breasted nuthatch
5 minutes	Steller's jay
3 minutes	northern flicker
3 minutes	unidentified low-pitch motor
1 minute	Canada goose
1 minute	unidentified songbird
1 minute	chickaree (or Douglas squirrel)

Yes, once again the sounds of aircraft dominated the hour. What a pity. Most of the aircraft were commercial jets, but there were also two turbo-prop cargo planes—that make a very distinct drone—and a helicopter.

The rest of the sounds were produced mostly by birds, with ravens and red-breasted nuthatches dominating the hour, which is typical at this time of year.

I mustn't neglect to mention, however, that eight of the sixty minutes were completely silent, except for the very distant roar of the McKenzie River in the valley just to the north of where I am sitting.

I wonder what sounds will be heard at this same spot, both 50 and 100 years from now? Will civilization as we know it still be around? Will aircraft still be around? How about ravens?

Only one thing is for sure: I will no longer be around then. But perhaps someone else who enjoys spending his time in the woods and listening to and appreciating the sounds around him—as well as moments of complete natural silence—will be able to compare his experience that day with my notes from today.

UNWANTED ABBREVIATIONS

I live in a state with a lovely name: Oregon. But with ever-increasing frequency, I see the name of the state reduced to just two capital letters, OR. Every state, of course, has a two-letter code introduced by the U.S. Postal Service in 1963, along with ZIP codes, ostensibly to expedite service. But many people have now adopted the two-letter abbreviations and use them regularly as substitutes for states' names.

Even in the obituaries of my local newspaper, these abbreviations have crept in. So-and-so "was born in Springfield, IL, was married in Springfield, MO, and then moved with his family to Springfield, OR, where he lived until his recent death." IL, MO, and OR are *not* the names of the states where this person lived; they are merely postal codes which, in my opinion, are completely inappropriate in an obituary.

Oregon is not the only state with an attractive name. In fact, I enjoy seeing and hearing the names of the other 49 states just as much. Most of them are of American Indian origin—for example, Wisconsin, Utah, Massachusetts, and Nebraska. Some names are New World versions of Old World places, such as New York and New Jersey. And several were named by early Spanish-speaking explorers and settlers, including Florida, Colorado, and Montana.

Then there's the wonderful Latin-derived name of the state where I grew up: Pennsylvania, or Penn's Woods, named for the family of its Quaker founder, William Penn, and *silva,* the Latin word for forest, because the state was once almost entirely forested. Finally, there are states—such as this one where I've lived most of my adult life—the names of which are of uncertain origin, although there are multiple interesting theories about their etymology.

Thankfully, most newspapers continue to use conventional abbreviations for the states, such as Oreg., Penna., Calif., and Mich. Why they ever even started to use these multi-lettered abbreviations, I don't know. Was it to save ink? Was it because some names like Massachusetts and Mississippi took up too much space or were likely to be misspelled? Was it because typesetters were in a hurry? The answer is unclear.

Interestingly, even when speaking, the citizens of one state commonly refer to their state by its two-letter abbreviation. Pennsylvanians say Pittsburgh, *pee-ay* or Philadelphia, *pee-ay*. (Pa. was of course one of the earlier abbreviations for Pennsylvania, along with Penn. and Penna., well before PA came along.) I know of no other state where this is done. No one says, for instance, that she is from Buffalo, *enn-why*, or from Sacramento, *see-ay*.

The use of abbreviations for place names has more recently spread to cities. Sure, Los Angeles has long been abbreviated LA and Philadelphia has been written as Phila.—again, for unclear reasons. But these days, many Oregonians, when referring in text to the state's largest city, write it as PDX—and occasionally even *say* it as *pee-dee-ex*—when in fact PDX is the three-letter code for Portland's airport, not the city itself. Will Eugene someday be called *ee-yoo-gee*, the same as its airport code? I hope not.

In the meantime, I'm running a one-man campaign to restore the use of all fifty states' full names, both when referring to them in text, as well as when addressing mail. After all, the U.S. Postal Service already has ZIP codes for everywhere in the U.S. Why does it also need to abbreviate the states' beautiful names?

These days, I proudly write out the whole word Pennsylvania—and waste a lot of ink, I suppose, and maybe even slow down the movement of the nation's mail—when sending a letter to my sister in Lancaster. And sometimes, for fun, I'll even write Penn's Woods instead of Pennsylvania, just to see what happens. So far, every such letter has been delivered. I suspect that post office employees (and their machines) simply ignore state names anymore—whether written out or abbreviated—and depend almost exclusively on ZIP codes to move the mail.

By the way, did you know that ZIP stands for Zone Improvement Plan?

LEAVING THE FOG BEHIND

Earlier this winter, when Eugene was experiencing day after day of heavy fog, I elected one day to escape the fog by taking the bus east into the McKenzie Valley of the Cascade Mountains, where I knew that the sun would be shining.

During a wintertime temperature inversion, the southern Willamette Valley—which includes the Eugene-Springfield area—often sits under a blanket of cold, damp fog while the rest of Western Oregon is bathed in warm sunshine. There are two ways to escape the fog: 1) by getting above it, which I can do by climbing 2,065-foot-high Spencer Butte on the south edge of Eugene, the summit of which is always out of the fog; or 2) by going *west* into the Coast Range, or *east* into the Cascades, both of which are also always fog-free during inversions.

This day, the bus left foggy Eugene Station, passed through foggy Springfield, and then headed through yet more fog into the McKenzie Valley. Just after crossing the McKenzie River for the first of two times during its sixty-mile-long route, the bus suddenly popped out of the fog and into the glorious sunshine. Seeing the deep blue sky above instead of the dreary gray of the fog simply made my heart sing. I broke into a broad smile and was on the verge of applauding, until I realized that hardly anyone else in the bus seemed to have noticed the change in atmosphere.

So I just giggled contentedly to myself, turned my face toward the sun, and recalled a similar experience many years ago when I lived in Bern, the capital of Switzerland. Bern is located in about the center of the *Mittelland* or central plateau of Switzerland—which includes two of Switzerland's other large cities, Geneva and Zürich. Like the Willamette Valley, the

Mittelland is surrounded by mountains, with the Alps to the south and the Jura to the north and northwest. During the winter and early spring, cold fog and low clouds sometimes blanket the area while the Alps are enjoying mild weather and sunshine. I'd gotten above the fog more than a few times during my stay in Bern by taking the train south to Zweisimmen in the Berner Oberland Alps, where I could ski cross-country under blue skies while Bern sulked all day in the fog.

Just as I have two options for escaping Eugene's fog—go *up* in elevation or go *out* of the immediate area—the Swiss who live in the Mittelland also have two options, one of which I've just mentioned. The second is to hop an Intercity train and head to the south side of the Alps, to Ticino (tee-CHEE-noh), the area of Switzerland that abuts northern Italy.

So one gray day, that's just what I did by taking a train from Zürich to Locarno. Although trains go up many of the alpine valleys in winter to ski resorts and in summer to provide access to hiking trails, most of those trains dead-end at the upper ends of the valleys. Intercity trains, on the other hand, go *through* the Alps in long tunnels.

My Locarno-bound train passed through many miles of lovely Mittelland countryside—although it looked a bit dreary in the fog—before entering the nine-mile-long Gotthard Tunnel. The passengers in my car, in typical Swiss fashion, were politely keeping to themselves by reading newspapers or books, looking out the window, or conversing in barely audible voices. People's attitudes are often a reflection of the weather, and because many of us on the train had spent the previous days under the Mittelland's gray skies, I suppose we were a bit dull and listless ourselves.

But after about ten minutes in the tunnel, the train popped out on the south side of the Alps and into the sunshine. Spontaneously, the passengers began applauding vigorously and smiling at each other and conversing excitedly. We'd escaped the cold and dreary Mittelland and were being embraced by the warm and sunny Ticino!

Locarno was just a few minutes away, and the joyful atmosphere in my car continued as we approached the city. When I got off the train in Locarno and walked outside the station, I found palm trees swaying in the breeze and huge beds of bright red tulips glowing brilliantly under deep blue skies. I felt like a new person! My train trip to Ticino was one of the most therapeutic I've ever taken.

WHITEY'S WORLD AND HOW IT WORKS

While I was working in the front yard late one afternoon, a young man walked by and, when I looked up and said hello, he returned my greeting, then stopped, turned toward me, and said, "I really like your place—it's the nicest house in the whole neighborhood!" I thanked him for his kind words, asked him where he lived, and said he was welcome to come into the yard and look around whenever he wanted. He said his name was Sereno and that he and his mom had recently moved into the house down at the corner.

When I told him, "Please, go check out the backyard and say hi to my hens," he hesitated briefly, then scooted up the entry boardwalk and headed for the backyard, while I continued my work. Only a minute or two later he came back out front and asked me point blank, "Why do you do this?" I wasn't sure what he meant, and was a bit taken aback. "Do what?" I asked. "Make such a beautiful yard, grow your own food, have solar panels on your roof . . . stuff like that."

After I'd paused for a moment to gather my thoughts, I replied, "Well, I guess I never thought about *why* I live like this. It just makes sense to want to care for this little piece of the planet in the most thoughtful way I know, and to grow as much of my own food as possible and produce at least some of the electricity I need right on-site instead of importing it from somewhere else. I also feel that, with more than seven billion of us now in the world, it's my personal responsibility to live with as small a 'footprint' as possible—without feeling, of course, like I'm depriving myself of a decent life."

Sereno looked me right in the eye, and said, "*Everybody* should live like this!" Then he turned away and continued on his way home.

Only a few weeks after my encounter with Sereno, one of the young students in the University of Oregon course I teach—The Nature of Eugene—asked me a similar question after I'd brought the class to see my house and yard during one of our off-campus field trips. In fact, Alec went a step farther and suggested that I write a "short essay" about how I live, and how my lifestyle has affected me as well as others. In light of the ongoing interest in how I live my life and how I care for my property—and also because I thought this self-examination would be a really good exercise for me—I decided to follow his suggestion.

The Facts of (Whitey's) Life

First of all, I probably should list some of the more significant aspects of my life that others apparently consider singular:

- I've never owned an automobile, and my property has neither a driveway nor a garage taking up precious space.
- My adjusted gross income averages $10,000 per year.
- I grow virtually all of my own fruits and vegetables, and raise chickens as well as bees.
- I pay no rent or mortgage.
- My passive-solar, 523-square-foot house with finished loft heats itself on cold, sunny winter days.
- With rooftop photovoltaic panels, I produce most of the electricity I use on an annual basis, although I cook and meet my supplemental space-heating needs with natural gas.
- I own no electronic devices—no mobile phone, no computer, no television, no DVD-player—but I do have a 25-year-old telephone that is tethered to a wall outlet.
- I have three bicycles: 1) a three-speed with baskets front and back for everyday use; 2) a twelve-speed mountain-type bike with trailer hitch and utility trailer for hauling heavy loads; and 3) a twelve-speed touring bike.
- I live alone and have no children.
- I wear several different hats in terms of what I "do" and do not believe in working (at least for money) full-time.
- I rarely eat out in restaurants—at most once or twice a year.

- I don't believe in vacations, paid or otherwise; at least part of every day should qualify as a holiday.
- I have no health insurance, and instead pay cash for the occasional medical attention I need.

Why I Live the Way I Do

Over the course of my life, I've observed closely how other people live—from the thriving Amish community in Lancaster County, Pennsylvania where I grew up, to so-called peasant cultures in Latin America—and decided what I liked and didn't like. Then I went about creating a life that would provide me with a high level of both satisfaction and contentment. A typical day needed to include a blend of work-for-pay and work-for-free; mental work and physical work; and time divided about equally between being indoors and being outdoors.

Most adults in our culture work full-time; that is, at least forty hours and five days per week. They work not necessarily because they love their work, but in order to pay for the roof over their heads, raise their kids, pay for the family car(s), pay for health care, and buy machines that are thought to make their lives easier. All the time that they spend working is of course time that is not spent "living"—enjoying time at their own discretion. And I knew that I wanted to *live* full-time instead of *work* full-time.

So I started by eliminating the items listed in the preceding paragraph: mortgage, kids, motor vehicles, health care and insurance, and labor-saving devices. If I didn't have any of these expenses, I wouldn't have to spend my precious time on the planet working to pay for those things.

I eliminated the mortgage by in essence inheriting a house. If our country had a stable population and each family had only two children, each child and his or her mate would therefore inherit a house or sufficient funds to purchase a modest house. That is, there would be a constant turnover of houses, from one generation to the next, as the older generation passed on and the younger generation took over that house—or its equivalent. It's that simple.

As much as I like kids and think I would be a good father, I elected to have no children. I firmly believe that the world's human population needs to be dramatically reduced, and the most effective way for me as an individual to contribute to that reduction is by choosing to be childless myself. Even without children of my own, I still feel like I have a significant effect on the lives of young people, because my university students are exposed to my beliefs and lifestyle in my courses, whether that exposure is purposeful or incidental.

The privately-owned motor vehicles were replaced by bicycles—and by largely eliminating my need for travel other than by bike and occasionally by bus or train.

My health care costs are extremely low due in part to my healthy lifestyle—eating good food, being physically active, spending a lot of time outdoors, and having a low-stress life. Moreover, I've been very fortunate indeed never to have had a serious illness or injury.

The machines I eliminated because I simply have no need for most of them. Although I do own a washing machine, I dry my clothes on a line. In the kitchen I supply all the power myself for stirring, beating, slicing, and so on—it's good for my upper body. And I can't stand the noise of anything with an engine, whether gas or electric.

With regard to electronic devices, the majority of them serve either to entertain us or to pick up the pace of our lives. But I've always been pretty much self-entertaining. And the last thing I want to do is speed up my life.

I also believe that machines are used most efficiently and effectively if they are *shared.* Why should everyone own a power lawnmower or pick-up truck or hot tub or whatever? Such machines and appliances sit idle for most of the time. I do use computers, but I depend on publicly-owned ones at the university libraries. That way, I'm sharing the machines with others, and I'm also keeping them at arm's length so I'm not tempted to overuse them. I try to limit my screen time to two hours per day.

Lastly, I've always thought that a labor-saving device or gadget should, well, save us time—time that we could then put to a higher use. Instead, any savings in time seems for most people to be filled with just more work.

Putting a Good Life Together

After quitting my Ph.D. program at the University of Wisconsin in the early 1980s, I thought about where I'd like to spend the rest of my life, and I chose Eugene, Oregon for five important reasons:

1. Most of the city is on the flat valley floor and getting around by bicycle is easy, so there is really no conceivable need for a car.
2. An excellent transit system—for a U.S. city of its size—provides an alternative to bicycling, should the need arise.
3. With its mild climate, cooling my house in summer and heating it in winter is relatively inexpensive—and having a year-round food garden is possible.
4. With a large public university, I have easy access to excellent libraries, a lovely, safe, and clean public park (the campus), a recreation center, and cultural events of interest (museums, lectures, etc.), all at no or very low cost.
5. The transit system includes a bus that takes me for just a dollar or two some sixty miles into the Cascade Mountains east of Eugene and drops me off in the Willamette National Forest. (Although I'm attracted to university towns in general—and Eugene in particular—for their many amenities, both solitude and quiet are also very important to me, so I must have an inexpensive way to escape on a regular basis.)

After moving to Eugene in 1983, I spent the next fifteen years putting together the essential pieces of the life I wanted. Except for a brief period in 1992 when I worked for the City of Eugene, I have never had a full-time job. In fact, at times, I have had as many as three part-time jobs concurrently—and still plenty of free time for myself.

Even with an annual income of only about $10,000, I am able some years to put as much as $4,000 of it into my savings, so I have a substantial amount of money that I can draw on during my older age or in the event of a medical emergency. Most of my annual savings, though, usually go back into maintaining and continually improving my house and garden. If I eventually retire, I expect to live largely off of my savings, since I don't believe that social security should be considered an entitlement—as it is by most Americans—especially for people who have sufficient other means of supporting themselves in their older age.

Where does my money *come* from? I teach two courses every year at the University of Oregon. I still have a couple of paying clients—from my former business as a consulting horticulturist and landscape designer—whose landscapes I care for. And I offer an annual program of about a dozen field classes in natural history through my very small OUT-OF-DOORS business.

How My Lifestyle Has Affected Me

The life I've created for myself is deeply satisfying. On a regular basis, I tell myself how fortunate I am, and how content I am with how things have worked out. I'm especially glad to have learned long ago the meaning of the word "enough" so I don't feel the constant need to acquire more money, a newer car, or a bigger house. The toaster I use was a wedding gift to my parents in 1943 and it still works fine, so why buy a new or different one?

Some people believe that leading a comparatively simple life like I do requires that one deprive oneself of certain things that one might otherwise want. But that has not been the case for me. I know the difference between wanting something and needing it, and my wants are even fewer than my needs. Before acquiring anything new, I always ask myself if I think my life will truly be any better if I purchase the item. If it won't, I don't buy it.

A perfect illustration of this is the number of gardening tools I own. Although garden centers offer scores (maybe even hundreds) of different tools to choose from, *all* of my gardening needs, both personally and for my clients, are met with just twelve tools:

- 3 digging tools: round-tip shovel, spade-fork, and trowel
- 4 cutting tools: pruning saw, lopper, sécateur (hand pruner), and grass-clippers
- 3 clean-up tools: leaf rake, broom, and scoop shovel
- 2 miscellaneous tools: wheelbarrow and push mower

Most of the personal benefits of my lifestyle are derived from the greater amount of "free time" that I have, since I don't have to work for money so many hours of the week to meet my needs. I get to spend at least one day every week alone in the woods. I have time to spend on my garden and my house, and at organizing (and re-organizing) my personal belongings. And I suppose I also have more time than most people for my "charitable work," from picking up litter around the neighborhood and keeping storm drains open, to organizing my popular *Nordic Film Series* on campus every year, and working to reduce noise and light pollution in my community.

Any negative effects of my lifestyle? Just one that I can think of. Because I live my life on a completely different financial plane than most people, when I occasionally need to purchase services from someone else— carpenter, doctor, lawyer—it is exceedingly expensive for me. Although I earn between $10 and $30 an hour for most of my own paid work, other professionals in my culture are accustomed to being paid $60 or $100 or more per hour. With their six-digit incomes, they are able to operate comfortably in the current system of inflated egos and salaries. But for someone like myself, with a barely *five*-digit income, it can create a hardship. Fortunately, I rarely need to use the services of these professionals, all of whom I consider vastly overpaid.

How My Lifestyle Has Affected Others

The way I live seems to attract a good bit of attention, especially when people learn how comparatively low my income is. I think that most people can tell how content I am with my life even without me saying so myself, and they wonder if there is perhaps something they might learn from me.

Lewis Mumford and other writers have stressed the importance of meeting one's very limited personal needs first—food, clothing, shelter—and then being able to spend the rest of one's time and life working (for free) to improve one's community and just enjoy one's own life. I think that this is the most important way I affect other people, again because I have the *time* available for such pursuits, time that has been made available to me simply by spending fewer hours of every week working for money.

Concluding Remarks

I don't want readers to think that this essay provides a blueprint for happiness for everyone. On the contrary, I recognize how difficult it is for most people to live within limits—*restraint is the greatest challenge!* We humans seem to just naturally want more of most everything: more shoes, more vacation days, more dessert, and more years in our lives. Throughout human history, there have always been those who chose to live with less and seek personal happiness instead of more stuff. But it's just not the kind of life most people can lead, without feeling deprived in some way—and that's a perfectly good reason for *not* living the way I do. But it works well for me, and there are certainly *some* aspects of my life that I know others can incorporate in their lives. But I accept and understand that the kind of life I lead is beyond the ability of most. I'm certainly not any better than anyone else because I live the way I do—I'm just different.

I am blessed to have been born with a good mind, and to have had good health for most of my life. Plus, I had parents who were both willing and able to help me purchase a modest house—by loaning me the funds, before their deaths, that would eventually become part of my inheritance. I have been fortunate in so many ways, and it's that good fortune—as well as my desire to live more purposefully, perhaps, than some people do—that has made possible this life that many observers seem to admire.

Good fortune notwithstanding, do I think everyone *should* live as I do? Of course not. Each person must determine for him or herself where on the broad economic spectrum of possible lifestyles he or she can find contentment. Some people (even here in the U.S.) are perfectly content with an income much lower than mine—and a house or apartment containing even fewer things. I admire them. And I know that I could do better myself, by even further reducing my so-called footprint without compromising my comfort. I certainly don't need as large a house as I happen to have, and I have in fact seriously considered finishing the small cottage in the back of my property, living there and renting the main house to someone else, or to a couple. However, because I've lived alone for so many years now, I doubt that I'd be comfortable sharing my property with others.

Maybe my own personal luxury is occupying an entire city lot all by myself. Even those of us who exercise restraint in our lives in many ways may still be living lives of excess in other ways.

THINGS WITH WINGS
Aural Snapshot No. 23

It's midday, sunny, and 50 degrees here at the 2,000-foot elevation in Oregon's West Cascades. I'm sitting in an open area next to a fifty-year-old stand of Douglas-firs, and thinking that it's a fine time for me to do an aural snapshot of what this area sounds like on the first day of spring—20 March 2014. As usual, I'll record on paper the different sounds I hear each minute during the course of a single hour—whether the sound occurs just once during the minute, is repetitive, or is constant.

After 60 minutes, during which I concentrated intensely on the task at hand, here are the results:

58 minutes	fly
29 minutes	tapping of a sapsucker
	(a kind of woodpecker)
22 minutes	robin
12 minutes	commercial jet
10 minutes	red crossbill
6 minutes	Steller's jay
4 minutes	raven
3 minutes	cargo plane
2 minutes	pileated woodpecker
1 minute	chickadee
1 minute	bee

Yes, over an entire hour, I heard only eleven different sounds other than the light breeze in the trees and distant Horse Creek in the canyon below.

And is it possible that I heard no sounds whatsoever from ground-based creatures? Indeed, every one of the eleven sounds came from an animal or a machine with wings. Life on Earth has come a very long way since the first creatures crawled out of the sea onto the land, and only much later acquired the ability to fly. And human beings took to the air just a little more than a century ago.

Surprisingly, the sound of aircraft dominated only a quarter of the hour. Because they can be heard on average here in the Cascades some 23 minutes of every hour—and I am unfortunately unable to escape their noise—I feel especially blessed today.

But I've simply had it with the sound of these buzzing flies! Thankfully, all I need to do to escape *their* noise is to get up and go find a nice spot in the deep shade of a nearby stand of old trees, as flies avoid the shade when they can be flitting around in the sunshine on a day like today.

My work for the day now finished—an hour of listening, and then the writing up of my results—off I go!

BALM OF GILEAD

It's the third week of May here in the West Cascades, where the new fronds of sword ferns are now nearly fully unfurled and the hermit warblers have been back for several weeks already. The temperature about midday is certainly in the mid-60s, yet it's snowing lightly. The flakes vary a great deal in size, from maybe a quarter of an inch across to some that are as wide as an inch and a half. But instead of floating more of less directly earthward, they seem at times to wander aimlessly among the tall moss-covered trunks of the broad-leafed trees above and around me.

The boughs of young hemlocks in the forest undercanopy are starting to accumulate a bit of the snowfall now, and in the tiny stream nearby, still pools have become nearly covered in white. Curiously, there's not a cloud in the sky, so the casual observer might well be puzzled by these events. But I'm not. I've been here other years about this time, and seen it snow before. The snow, of course, is the cottony fluff of the cottonwood trees high above me, which bloomed earlier this spring and are now releasing their tiny seeds. Each seed is attached to a small piece of "cotton." The larger pieces of fluff floating by me have multiple seeds in them with "conjoined" fluff.

Not all of the cottonwoods in this stand are releasing seed-bearing fluff right now, as many of the trees are male. They shed their pollen back in March, which was carried by the wind to fertilize the flowers on the female trees. The pollen-bearing organs of the male trees then fell off, but the female organs remained on the trees until the seeds matured. By mid-June, when there will be no more cotton to shed nor seeds to launch into the clear blue sky, they'll drop to the ground as well, having completed their reproductive duty for this year.

I've always found this stand of trees especially attractive, as it's composed almost entirely of broad-leafed trees: cottonwoods, for the most part, but also quite a few red alders and bigleaf maples. Most of the trees are about my age or a little older, having colonized this moist, valley-bottom site following a wildfire sometime in the mid-1940s. I'm reminded of the hardwood forests of southeastern Pennsylvania, where I grew up, as the light that comes through the leafy canopy here is similar to that which filters through the forest canopy where I spent some of the best days of my youth. The quality of the light in a stand of broad-leafed trees is very different from that which reaches the forest floor in a stand of conifers— which dominate most of the landscape of western Oregon—because the light passes *through* the thin, broad leaves, rather than being *blocked* by the thicker, darker needles of native conifers.

When cottonwood trees first break bud in early spring and begin to leaf out, this area is fragrant with the sweet smell of the propolis-like compound which coats the new leaves. Even now, less than a month from the summer solstice, the lovely scent persists. Whenever I smell it, it makes me smile and sigh, as it's truly aroma-therapeutic. That is, smelling it makes me feel good.

Early Euro-Americans in this region called these trees Balm of Gilead, a biblical reference to a possibly related tree—that is, a cottonwood or poplar—that likely grew in the Middle East, the scent of which was restorative or "balmy." These days, the word balmy is often used to refer to a warm winter day among a long string of more seasonably cold ones. But the word properly refers more to the *scent* of the air than its temperature.

In fact, it's more than just the scent of the Balm of Gilead that is restorative. Resin from the tree's buds is highly medicinal. It is antibacterial, antifungal, and mildly analgesic, and is an ingredient in cough syrups and first-aid salves used by herbalists to heal small wounds, cuts, and scrapes.

Although most everyone these days calls these fragrant and cotton-producing trees cottonwoods, a few old-timers—especially in rural areas of western Oregon—still refer to them as "bam" trees. The word "bam" is clearly a diminutive of "Balm of Gilead" or simply "balm" trees, and *b-a-l-m* just became *b-a-m* over time. The trees' contemporary name, cottonwood, certainly reflects a notable characteristic of the species—the cottony masses that disseminate its seeds—but its now-archaic name, Balm of Gilead, still holds a special and aromatic place in my heart.

A FOUR-COURSE BREAKFAST
IN A FIVE-STAR RESTAURANT

I'm back in the woods of the West Cascades once again for a few days of fresh air, quiet, and solitude. Who could ask for more?

Following a delicious night's sleep, I awoke to sunshine streaming into the tent, and wondered to myself what I might make of the day. Following yesterday's strenuous climb—almost 2,500 feet vertical gain in just over two miles of trail—I decided to make this a rest day.

After getting water at a nearby spring, I headed up the hill on the little-used trail and, in less than a half-mile, found just the right spot to have breakfast. I set up my little kitchen counter—a plastic file-folder holder (that I'm also using at the moment as my writing desk)—and proceeded to light my stove and bring a pot of tea water to a boil.

Once the bag of double-bergamot Earl Grey was steeping nicely, I put a second pot on with just a cup of water in it, and brought it to a boil as well. Then I added my oatmeal—which I'd pre-mixed at home (oats, raisins, dried apples, walnuts, and salt)—and let it simmer until done, about fifteen minutes here at the 3,000-foot elevation.

While my oatmeal "rested" after being cooked, I prepared my second course by mixing a little canned evaporated milk and an egg. Once the butter was sizzling in the frying pan, I added the egg-milk mixture and then relaxed to enjoy my oatmeal, to which I'd added evaporated milk, a little butter, and cinnamon.

Just before folding over my omelet-to-be, I sprinkled it with salt and pepper, and placed several thin slices of sharp cheddar on top of it. When it was finally done, I lowered the heat and turned my attention toward appreciating my second course: a delicious cheese omelet.

Then the frying pan went back on the burner, which I'd turned back up, and I toasted half of a bagel, split in two, in butter. When it was just right, I topped the two pieces with cherry jam and enjoyed my third course, along with what remained of the evaporated milk.

Finally, I lifted the now-ready pot of tea onto my lap—atop one of my mittens that also serves as a potholder—and took one quarter of a toffee-bar (a purchased pastry) from my special little plastic pastry container, and sat back to enjoy my fourth and final course while a little dishwater heated up on the stove.

Once the dishes had been washed in hot, soapy water, then rinsed and laid out to air-dry, I leaned back with my hands clasped behind my head and smiled. I couldn't imagine any restaurant anywhere that could be lovelier than the one where I'd just had my delicious breakfast: Fresh air, a table for one with a view of the entire valley below and the mountains beyond, no annoying conversations from neighboring tables, and no irritating music from overhead speakers. Who could ask for more?

AN AROMATIC LITTLE FOREST DENIZEN

Of all the creatures I've met through the years in western Oregon's forests, none is more curious or intriguing than a little many-legged invertebrate that crawls around on mossy forest floors. It's extremely common, especially in spring and early summer, yet few Oregonians are familiar with it.

Although it looks a bit like a centipede—being long and slender and segmented, with pairs of legs on each segment—it is actually a species of *millipede*. Centipedes, for you beginners, have only a single pair of legs per body segment, while millipedes have two pairs per segment.

I've always associated this millipede species with forest environments, but in recent years, I've seen them regularly in my yard in town, as well. Could it be that I just didn't notice them before? Or have they recently expanded their range into more urban areas? I don't know. And no one else seems to know much about these "boring" critters—or cares about them. But I do.

I don't recall the first time I saw this millipede, but it's certainly at least two decades ago. They're hard to miss as they amble among the mosses and other plants on the forest floor: they are about two inches long, shiny black on top, and down each side of their segmented bodies is a line of orange dots, two per segment (one on each side).

Besides their attractive and interesting countenances, this species of millipede has a very, very special attribute. Again, I don't recall when I might have discovered this, but at some point, I picked one of them up to look at it more closely—they immediately curl up in a self-defense

34

posture—and after I put it back down, I must have touched my fingers to my nose. And I smelled something wonderful: almond paste or almond extract! I couldn't believe it at first, but yes, it was the millipede that had left the scent on my fingers.

Because almond paste is an ingredient in marzipan—often used in European confections, inside a chocolate coating—I decided to call my new friends marzipan millipedes. Curiously, few people, including naturalists who should know better, are aware of this millipede's remarkable trait. I've never seen even the millipede itself mentioned in Pacific Northwest natural history texts and field guides, and definitely not its marzipan aroma. Why is this?

As abundant as marzipan millipedes are in local forests, they lead quite solitary lives most of the time. You find one here, you see one there; and I've only rarely seen them mating. But one summer day in the Coast Range west of Eugene, not far from Triangle Lake, I witnessed a remarkable procession of millipedes. I'd stopped my vehicle along a quiet forest road, and on my way to a grassy spot nearby to have my picnic lunch, I noticed in the moist ditch along the gravel road an amazing sight. Countless thousands of marzipan millipedes were crawling along the bottom of the shaded ditch, all headed in the same direction.

When I related my experience in a letter to my friend, Kurt—who lived in Low Pass in the Coast Range and wandered widely in the surrounding forests—he responded in his next letter to me that I had witnessed the first ever Million Millipede March for Environmental Sanity. He suggested that, finally, Mother Nature's creatures were banding together and marching in public to bring attention to all of the environmental degradation caused by humans. I found Kurt's response amusing, but I'm still puzzled by what I saw that extra-special day in the Coast Range.

Whenever I have the opportunity, I make an effort to enlighten others about my marzipan millipede buddies. Interestingly, many people—especially women, for some reason—are reluctant to even touch the millipedes, and use words such as "gross" and "creepy-crawly" and "icky" in reference to these completely harmless creatures. But for those who are willing to touch the aromatic invertebrates, their responses are always the same: "Oh, it smells so good!" How could one *not* love marzipan millipedes, once you've been properly introduced?

WHITE-FLOWER WEEK

It's almost the end of May here in Oregon's West Cascades, where an annual celebration is occurring that few people seem to know or care about. Like the Christians' Easter, the timing of this celebration varies from year to year, depending in this case on how early or late spring arrives. The events that occur over the course of a year—from the opening of the first tiger lily bud, to the return of the Swainson's thrushes from their wintering grounds—always take place in the same sequence. But in any given year, that sequence can shift forward or backward as much as two weeks from the long-term average, due largely to daily temperatures, especially those of late winter and spring. For example, warmer than usual temperatures in February or March cause the sequence to begin earlier; and colder than usual temperatures in April or May push all the events later into the year.

Once a person is aware of what's going on around him, the year is an endless series of these celebrations. Almost a month ago already, I celebrated Hermit Warbler Week, when that species of songbird returned here in large flocks and seemingly overnight. The warblers will breed in this area through early summer, then head back south later in the season. And Hermit Warbler Week happens to coincide almost exactly with Pacific Slope Flycatcher Week, as the two species of birds almost always return within a few days of each other.

But back to White-Flower Week, which is a particularly special time of year when many white-flowered plants bloom simultaneously. One of the most common here at an elevation of about 2,000 feet is starflower (*Trientalis major*), a delicate little bloom about a half-inch across, with six or so pointed white (or occasionally light pink) petals. The single flower arises from a whorl of four to seven leaves atop a solitary stem. Starflower grows in groups of maybe a dozen to as many as hundreds of plants, all connected underground by rhizomes or underground stems. So it's really one plant with many heads of solitary flowers. Starflower grows on shady or sunny sites, but is most common on the former.

On sunny sites, both wild strawberry and whipple-vine can also be seen blooming. Like the cultivated strawberry, the flower of wild strawberry (*Fragaria virginiana*) has five white petals with rounded tips, and the plant itself has leaves composed of three toothed leaflets. Unlike starflower, it spreads *above* the ground via stolons, creating little neighborhoods of strawberry plants, all of which are connected to each other. Whipple-vine (*Whipplea modesta*), too, forms a dense mat, often on sunny slopes, from which it raises its little heads of a dozen or so white-petaled flowers. The leaves of whipple-vine are arranged opposite one another along the plant's stems which creep across the ground, enlarging the mat from one year to the next.

The fourth white-flowered plant joining in the celebration this week is red-stem ceanothus (*Ceanothus sanguineus*). This large, sparsely-leafed shrub is found on sunny sites and can reach a height of ten feet or more. Right now, it's covered with showy clusters of creamy-white flowers. The clusters are up to three inches long and two inches across, but the individual flowers are quite tiny.

Other white-flowered plants blooming now include the Columbia windflower (*Anemone deltoidea*) and the yellow-leaf iris (*Iris chrysophylla*), both of which tend to grow and flower best on the edges of woodlands, where they get very good light but no direct sun—at least not for very long periods.

There is also a showy *pink*-flowered shrub, the native Pacific rhododendron (*Rhododendron macrophyllum*), that has begun to bloom and certainly deserves its own annual celebration. And there are white-flowered plants that bloomed *earlier* (e.g., trillium) and some that will bloom *later* (e.g., Cascades lily), but only during White-Flower Week do so *many* plants with white blooms come into flower. It's an event worth celebrating, especially if you have blond hair and your nickname is Whitey!

A VISIT TO TIRE MOUNTAIN

I'd been to Tire Mountain only once before—perhaps five years ago—and was at the time impressed beyond words with the wildflower-filled meadows of this West Cascades peak near Oakridge. But this year, I was going to be teaching an all-day field class there, so I thought I should visit the area again, just to re-familiarize myself with the trail and decide what stops I wanted to make along the trail to discuss the area's natural history.

The first time I'd visited Tire Mountain, a friend and I drove there together. This time, I wanted to go alone and, since I don't own a car, I thought first of borrowing a car from a friend, or possibly renting one. After giving the matter of transportation a little more thought, I decided instead to forego the use of a single-occupant vehicle altogether and instead combine bus and bicycle to reach my destination.

For years, I'd heard about the Diamond Express bus that daily shuttles commuters between the Oakridge/Westfir area and Eugene/Springfield, and I'd occasionally seen the bus picking up passengers near 11th and Willamette in downtown Eugene. For a one-way fare of only $2.50, the bus would take my bike and me from Eugene to Westfir, a distance of about forty miles, and I'd bike the rest of the way to the trailhead.

So on Wednesday morning, June 11, 2014, I was at the bus stop downtown plenty early, to be sure there would be a space in the bus's bike rack for my bike. But I hadn't needed to worry about that, as I was the only passenger waiting for the 7:45 a.m. bus! Like most commuter transit, the routes are heavily used in one direction—inbound from Oakridge to Eugene—in the morning, and in the opposite direction in late afternoon, when workers are headed back home for the evening.

It was a beautiful ride to Westfir, and I could enjoy the passing landscape to its fullest as my "private chauffeur" carried me along the Middle Fork Willamette River, past Dexter and Lookout Point reservoirs, and into the Cascades. When I got off at the Westfir Middle School, it wasn't even mid-morning yet, and I headed north into the small town of Westfir where I stopped only briefly at the big red Office Bridge—"Lane County's Longest Covered Bridge"—before following the North Fork Middle Fork Willamette River (that's its real name) farther into the mountains.

I'd planned to have my breakfast along the North Fork and found just the perfect spot among some large, smooth boulders on the west side of the river, just as the sun began to peek over the high ridge to the east. After a quick dip in the river to refresh myself, I settled down on a flat-topped boulder to enjoy my müesli, orange juice, and hot tea.

After that, my "work day" really began. Starting at an elevation of only 1,200 feet down by the North Fork, I had some six miles of steep gravel road ahead of me—forest road 1912—and a relatively heavy twelve-speed bike to take up the hill with me. I didn't pedal very far before I realized it would be almost as fast, and a lot easier, to simply push/pull the bike along with me as I walked, at least along the steepest parts of the road.

I ended up walking probably five of the six miles, and was passed by only two vehicles, both of them toting bikes and bikers up the hill. I'd been told that the trail I was headed for was popular with mountain bikers, but I didn't expect much traffic on a weekday. And yes, I couldn't help but feel just a little smug as those vanloads of bikers—most of them only a fraction of my age—drove past 61-year-old me as I pushed my bike up the hill.

Some two and a half hours after leaving the North Fork, I reached the trailhead for the Alpine Trail at an elevation of 3,800 feet, and hid my bike in the woods nearby before grabbing my daypack and heading up the trail.

After passing through an area that had been logged and re-forested decades ago, I reached a stand of huge Douglas-firs, some of which were clearly several centuries old. Only minutes later, I broke out into the first flower-filled meadow, a damp one on a northeast-facing slope, with western columbine, Sitka valerian, and maidenhair fern, along with many other wildflowers.

Only a few steps later, I came back out of a forested stretch of the trail onto a dry, east-facing, steeply sloping meadow that was just covered with wildflowers—but of altogether different species from the first, wetter meadow. After the brief climb at the beginning, the trail had leveled out and was incredibly easy to hike. One meadow succeeded the next, each one seeming to outdo its predecessor in terms of its size as well as the abundance and diversity of flower species. And the views toward snow-covered Diamond Peak to the southeast and The Three Sisters to the northeast were splendid under clear skies.

After only thirty minutes or so, I reached the junction with the Tire Mountain trail, which looped me back along the *west* side of the same ridge whose *east* slope the Alpine Trail had followed. More wonderful forest, and more lovely meadows. By then, it was lunchtime and I hiked up into one of the steep, west-facing meadows and found a shady spot beneath a bigleaf maple right at the meadow's edge. It was the perfect lunch spot, with not another soul around, and a view across the meadow and toward distant valleys and ridges to the southwest.

Although a nap would have been nice, I didn't have time to dawdle, as the last Diamond Express bus back to Eugene would leave Westfir Middle School at 4:20 p.m., and even though it was downhill all the way back, I still had almost 15 miles to pedal. But instead of retracing my steps to the trailhead where I'd begun, I decided to hike a little farther along the Tire Mountain trail to a saddle, then go cross-country through the woods, down to an abandoned forest road (the 1911) that would lead me back to my bike.

I thought it would be a shortcut, but I was wrong. The steep descent through the open woods—the forest floor richly carpeted with clover-like Oregon oxalis—was relatively easy at first. But descending that steep a slope was hard on my aging knees, and of course by then I was starting to panic a wee bit, when I realized I might have bitten off more than I could comfortably chew. But I certainly wasn't about to go back upslope to the trail, so onward!

Just before reaching the little road, I had to negotiate an incredible pile of fallen conifers, like giant pick-up sticks that someone had forgotten to pick up. It was brutal, as young western hemlocks grew densely among the rotting logs, so I was fighting a steep slope and dense young trees at the same time that I was having to go over and under the many huge logs.

When I finally reached the gravel road, I was a sweaty and dirty mess, but relieved to know that my bike would be just around the corner. Or would it not be? Indeed, the walk back up the road to my bike was much, much longer than I'd anticipated, and it was all uphill. Thankfully, the scenery along it was gorgeous, especially the masses of wildflowers, with particularly extensive stands of goatsbeard on the north-facing cut-banks along the road.

As I walked along the road, I kept thinking, "Ah, just around the next curve will be my bike!" And then there'd be yet another curve. I'm a really good map reader and cross-country hiker, so I was—and still am—puzzled how I could be so far off in estimating the distance back to my bike. But I finally reached it and when I looked at my watch, realized I had a little less than an hour to get down the hill, on to Westfir, and then the bus stop at the middle school.

I decided to go back down a different way—following the 1910 road, which I thought would be a little gentler descent than the road I'd come up on. Nothing is worse than biking downhill on a gravel road when you're in a hurry, so I knew I had to be extremely careful, yet I still had to catch that 4:20 bus.

My descent of the 1910 road was without incident, thankfully, and through lovely forest—a combination of both first- and second-growth conifers. And I didn't encounter any other vehicles or bikes along the way. When I finally could glimpse the North Fork through the trees, I let out a whoop. But I still had a ways to go.

With no time for my longed-for afternoon swim in the North Fork—following my hot-and-sweaty hike out—I crossed the concrete bridge to the paved Aufderheide Drive (forest road 19) that I'd come up on earlier in the day, and then turned south toward Westfir. All downhill for three miles, almost there! But it was mid-afternoon and, as usually occurs in the Cascades on warm, sunny days, a strong up-canyon wind had developed and was blowing right in my face. I'm sorry, but I cursed that wind—that on other days and in other locations I'd praised as it carried me *up* a hill instead—because I simply couldn't miss my bus.

Those few last miles seemed to take forever, and because of the wind, I had to keep my head down low and my eyes on the painted white fogline along the edge of the asphalt, both to better buck the wind and also because the road surface—which had been chip-sealed a few years before—was much too rough for biking, whereas the many layers of paint on the fogline were quite smooth for riding. I finally reached Westfir, where I'd planned to stop for ice cream at the little grocery. But I had to forego that treat, as well, as it was after 4 o'clock already and I still had a couple of miles to go. As I crossed the bridge over the Middle Fork and approached the school, I began to settle down, as it was 4:12—eight minutes yet until bus time. I'd made it.

At the bus stop, I unloaded my gear from my bike, took a swig of much-needed water, got out my bus pass, and kept my eyes on the approach road, in anticipation of my ride home. At 4:15, there was still no sign of the bus. Uh-oh. The morning driver had told me it was best to be a few minutes early at the stop, as a driver occasionally will leave the stop early if no one is there. I thought at the time, "They can't leave before the scheduled time!" But I said nothing to him.

There I was, tired beyond belief from the climb, the hike, the walk out, the descent, the headwind—and no swim and no ice cream!—and I was looking at being stranded upriver overnight. I considered my options, including biking to nearby Oakridge to stay in the hostel I'd heard good things about. But I decided instead to repack my bike and pedal only a quarter of a mile or so to the U.S. Forest Service Middle Fork Ranger Station, where I might get a ride back to town with someone getting off work at 4:30, who had a pick-up truck I could put my bike in.

At 4:19, just as I was pedaling back out the school's driveway to the Westfir Road, I saw the bus round the corner and start across the Middle Fork bridge toward me. Anger and disappointment immediately turned to elation, and I hurried back to the bus stop to unpack again and get ready to board.

I was so very happy to get on that bus—and was again one of only a few passengers on the afternoon town-bound run. After settling into my nicely cushioned seat, I enjoyed the ride home immensely, while counting my blessings the entire way back to Eugene for having successfully completed my little adventure that had turned out to be a bit bigger than I'd anticipated.

NATURE ROLLS OUT THE PINK CARPET FOR ME

I always feel welcome whenever I visit the woods. It's my natural habitat, after all, and I consider the forest's full-time residents—from marzipan millipedes to Roosevelt elk—to be my good friends. But on some days and at some seasons, the welcome is especially impressive. Today is one of those days.

The area where I like to spend my time has no maintained trails, so I get around using animal trails or occasionally forest roads, and by "bush-whacking" where I just make my way through the forest by climbing over logs and pushing branches out of the way. Stands of trees vary greatly in their accessibility, as the forest floor may be carpeted in places with tall shrubs such as vine maple and rhododendron which can create nearly impenetrable thickets. Conversely, some stands are almost park-like, and walking through them is a pleasure.

Like the other large animals who live here, I take the easy way out when offered a choice, so I tend to simply avoid shrub thickets and instead walk around them. But when I was confronted earlier today with a dense stand of Pacific rhododendron (*Rhododendron macrophyllum*), the stand appeared unusually welcoming, as the mossy forest floor was carpeted in pink flowers that had fallen from the tall shrubs overhead. Because the past few days have been unseasonably cool and damp, the fallen flowers hadn't even wilted. They looked almost as perky as they were when still attached to the tips of the evergreen shrub's branches last week, when they were at their peak of showiness.

Rhododendrons have what are called *gamopetalous* flowers. That is, instead of the petals falling off separately when they're spent—as they do, for example, in roses and tulips—the rhododendron's five petals are joined at the base, and the entire flower drops off as a unit. Once it reaches the ground, then, it still looks like a perfectly good flower, at least until it wilts or dries out.

Before entering the thicket, I thought of how some cultures spread flower petals on the ground as a member of royalty passes by, or for a newly-married couple to walk on. I felt honored that the rhododendrons appeared to have set the stage for *my* passing-by, having rolled out the pink carpet, so to speak. With a nod to my welcoming committee, the rhododendrons, I took my first step into the thicket and, wearing a broad smile, slowly proceeded to the other side some forty feet away.

It was the most ceremonious entry I've ever made into my sylvan refuge, where I spend at least one day every week. And it was a fitting start to what has turned out to be an unusually lovely June day.

AFTER THE DAWN CHORUS

I make a special effort every year around the summer solstice to get away to the woods for a few days. By that time, all of western Oregon's Neotropical migrants—birds that spend the warm months here, and then winter anywhere between California and South America—have finally returned for the summer. The last arrivals are always the nighthawks, which don't get here most years until the first week in June.

The focus of these birds is on raising their families, and since most of them are territorial, the breeding season, especially the early part, is spent on staking out territories and marking them with song. Although some songbirds sing throughout the day, others are heard mostly in the morning, just after dawn, and a few sing at both dawn and dusk.

Early on my second morning here, when it was barely light, I awoke to hear the *peent* sound of the nighthawks. They're not hawks at all, but are related to whippoorwills and, like those birds, are active mostly at twilight, feeding on insects while flying a few hundred feet above the ground. After a sequence of maybe a dozen *peent* sounds, a nighthawk will briefly be quiet, and then go into a dive that ends with a spectacularly loud *whoosh* sound as it pulls out of the dive just above the ground. It was the nighthawk's *whoosh* sounds that had awakened me.

Soon, they were joined by the tweets and trills and warbles and wheezes of a dozen other species, including spotted towhees, several species of warblers, and both hermit and Swainson's thrushes. I just lay in my tent and enjoyed all the singing—a human audience of one, as far as I knew.

Eventually, things settled down as the sun rose higher in the east. I'd fallen back asleep for a while, but then awoke again, fully rested and ready to hike the mile or so to where I would cook my breakfast. As I was getting my things together for the day, inside my tent, and packing my pack—I take absolutely everything with me except my tent, sleeping pad, and sleeping bag—I was startled by a loud crash nearby, like a large branch being broken. That was followed by ripping sounds and more branches breaking. What on earth?

The sounds were coming from just down the hill from my tent site, to the north, some fifty yards away. My tent was in an open area at the end of an abandoned logging road, but it was surrounded by a young stand of twenty-year-old Douglas-firs where the ground was densely covered with bracken (a sun-loving fern) taller than I am. So, once I stepped outside my tent, even though I could look toward the source of the noise, I could see nothing. But I knew very well what was going on: a black bear was stripping the bark off a young conifer, to reach the nutritious cambium layer just beneath the bark. I've seen evidence of this springtime foraging behavior of bears countless times in the past, but I'd never witnessed it occurring, either visually or aurally.

The noise continued for maybe five minutes, and then it was quiet. Where would the bear go next? I picked up my hiking stick—the closest thing I have to a weapon—and, adrenalin going and pulse faster than usual, I stood on the back side of my tent and waited. Nothing. I knew the bear hadn't fallen asleep—they do little more than forage 24 hours a day at this time of year—but where was it? Gulp.

I'm not afraid of bears, as my several face-to-face encounters with them in this area in the past have always ended with them running away from me as fast as their paws could carry them. These are wild bears that are not accustomed to being around humans, and because they are hunted in Oregon, most bears seem to know that the sight or sound of humans is to be avoided. Still, I'm always just a little uncomfortable when I know a bear's around, and I want to give them as much space as possible.

Hearing nothing more, I continued packing, and was almost ready to leave my camp for the day when, CRASH! This time, the noise came from the east, so the bear had made its way there by following the contour of the hill, rather than coming up and over the little knoll where my tent and I were. More crashing and ripping, as another young tree was being decorticated. Then silence.

I stood quietly and faced east-southeast with my "big ears"—my hands cupped by my ears to amplify any sounds. I could hear the swishing of ferns as the animal made its way around to the south of me, and then nothing more. I suspect the bear left the young fir stand and moved into the very open older stand just beyond, where its movement would be inaudible to me.

I'm just glad the bear didn't show up during the dawn chorus. Unlike the exceedingly talented birds, the furry percussionist seemed to have no sense of rhythm whatsoever.

A STORY OF TWO TOWHEADS

When I moved to Nantes, France in the mid-1970s, I underwent a variety of culture shocks, from being immersed in a language I was not yet fluent in, to living in a large, noisy city filled with cars that were unequipped with pollution-control devices. I'd moved to France from northern Sweden, where the air was pure and I worked on a small dairy farm in a quiet, rural setting. The contrast couldn't have been greater.

But another factor that contributed to almost daily headaches during my first months in France was the cigarette smoking. Back then, smoking was still a mostly accepted habit, both in the U.S. and in France. However, I had very few American friends who smoked, whereas the majority of the new friends I made in France did smoke. In the U.S., it was acceptable for me to ask a friend not to smoke when we were together, but in France, especially as a foreigner, I really couldn't do the same.

Less than two months after arriving in Nantes, I met a young man my age named Joël who would over time become my best French friend—and my best friend in life. Joël was studying architecture at the university in Nantes. We quickly became fast friends for several reasons, one of which might seem rather superficial. Joël's family was from Normandy—where the fair-haired Vikings had left more than footprints in the sand almost a thousand years before—and he was, like me, a first-class towhead.

Very blond men were a rarity in Nantes and we really stood out in a crowd. Joël was accustomed to being stared at, and I was by that time getting somewhat used to it myself. When a mutual friend, Frank, introduced us because he thought we had interests in common—urban design, the natural environment, etc.—he couldn't have been more right. But besides our shared interests, the fact that we were both towheads clearly contributed to the bond which soon developed.

Over the next few months, I spent as much time as possible with my new friend. I was working full time as a horticulturist and landscape architect for the Nantes parks department, but Joël and I were able to share many of our meals at the university dining hall, and frequently got together evenings or weekends to talk—with friends, or just the two of us. Of course, cigarette smoking was part of most every social occasion. I'd made it clear to Joël that I didn't care for smoking, but I didn't pester him about it. It was just a fact of life, and one of very few differences we had.

After about six months in Nantes, I decided to use some of the very generous vacation time that my job provided, and spend ten days hitchhiking to Scotland with Joël, who was on spring break. I don't recall how we decided on that destination, but neither of us had ever been to Great Britain before, and I was familiar with the song about "the bonny, bonny banks of Loch Lomond" in Scotland, so that's where we headed.

The first day, we made it as far as Roscoff on the north coast of Brittany, where we caught an overnight ferry to Plymouth, England. As the ferry approached the port just after dawn the following morning, it was snowing hard, and we asked ourselves if maybe we should have waited until later in the season to visit the British Isles. But we soldiered on, and our thumbs quickly carried us northward. More than a few times, the people who stopped to pick us up later revealed to us that they thought we two blonds were from Denmark or Sweden, and by stopping for us, they were simply demonstrating British hospitality for foreign visitors.

Over the months we'd known each other, Joël had considerately stopped smoking when just the two of us were together. And during our trip, we were together constantly, so I didn't think anything was out of the ordinary when I didn't see him smoking. Still, I thought I might occasionally get a glimpse of that familiar blue pack of Gauloises that he always carried with him. But I never did.

It was Easter-time and although there was still snow atop the lovely mountains of Scotland, bright yellow daffodils already filled the window-boxes in Glasgow. We two had a splendid time exploring the country, staying in rural bed-and-breakfasts, climbing the mountain slopes above Loch Lomond, and of course just enjoying each other's company.

But it wasn't until we were on the ferry back to France that Joël acknowledged to me that he had decided to quit smoking before we left France, and he'd never smoked a single Gauloise during our trip. Indeed, after our return from Scotland to Nantes, Joël never again smoked. It was the best gift my best friend could ever have given me. But Joël has ever since maintained that it was *I* who gave *him* the gift of a tobacco-free life— both by my example, being a non-smoker myself, as well as by taking him away from his cigarette-smoking friends and his Gauloises for more than a week, to enjoy the bracing and pure air of Scotland in the early spring.

A MIDSUMMER'S MORN
Aural Snapshot No. 24

One of the outstanding features of Oregon's forests is their silence. For much of the year, entire minutes—and sometimes several or more consecutive minutes—go by without a single sound being heard. If one is near a stream or if the wind is blowing, those sounds are of course audible. But the sounds of birds, insects, mammals, and machines are absent.

It's not like this elsewhere in the world. East of North America's Great Plains, for example, the hardwood forests of the temperate zone are full of sounds from mid-spring until well into fall. Only in late fall and winter do these forests fall silent, after most species of birds have migrated south for the winter, and insects have become dormant. During the growing season, however, a symphony of insects and birds performs day and night most places.

And in tropical forests, where the diversity of both plants and animals is so much higher and temperatures are mild year-round, the sounds of life can at times be almost deafening.

So this morning, 12 July 2014, I decided to do another one of my aural snapshots where I record everything I hear during an entire hour. For each minute, I noted each sound (if any) that I heard, whether the sound occurred just once during that minute, or was repetitive or constant. The only sounds I discounted were the burbling little creek nearby, occasional water drops falling from the forest's upper canopy—from last night's light rain—and an intermittent and very light breeze which now and again fluttered the foliage of nearby bigleaf maples. My location was only a couple of miles east of McKenzie Bridge, at an elevation of about 1,700 feet.

Here is the end-of-the-hour tally, in decreasing order of how many minutes of the hour included that particular sound:

12 minutes	fly
11 minutes	raven
10 minutes	chickaree (or Douglas squirrel)
9 minutes	commercial jet
8 minutes	Steller's jay
5 minutes	cargo plane
3 minutes	gnat
2 minutes	red crossbills
2 minutes	falling conifer needles
1 minute	mosquito
1 minute	vehicle going past on nearby road
1 minute	bee
1 minute	sound of unidentified bird's wings

That's a total of only 67 "sound-minutes" for the entire hour, or an average of slightly more than one source of sound per minute. Indeed, the highest number of different sounds heard in any one minute was just four, when I heard a commercial jet, a Steller's jay, a raven, and a chickaree (a kind of squirrel). Moreover, 17 of the 60 minutes were completely silent!

Only a month ago, things were quite different as it was the peak of the breeding season for most birds. But now that it's midsummer, those birds no longer need to advertise for mates or announce their territorial borders. So the forest is mostly very quiet again.

That's the principal reason I spend so much time in the West Cascades. As much as I enjoy hearing birds and insects and other natural sounds, I come here more specifically to experience the sound of silence that I love so very much. And in the conifer-dominated forests of the Northwest, I can enjoy that silence almost year-round.

LANE COUNTY'S NORTHWEST CORNER

The swells of an incoming tide are booming loudly just below me as they are forced through a sea-level cave of the highest near-shore eminence here at Captain Cook Point. A broad, water-filled chasm separates the mainland where I'm sitting from that hundred-foot-high hump of basalt which is home only to a thin mat of grasses, seaside angelica, and other hardy wildflowers of Oregon's littoral—the seaside strip that stretches from the Columbia River to the California border.

About halfway between Gwynn Creek and here, I stopped to make my breakfast atop a little volcanic shelf at the base of the cliff, which afforded a pleasant view of my surroundings. Breakfast consisted of four tiny pancakes—cooked in the frying pan of my Swedish-made Svea Optimus camp stove, and topped with butter and blackberry jam—plus a pot of tea.

My friend Robin and I spent a peaceful night at Horse Creek Campground, a few miles up into the hills and inland from the coast highway. The campground is designed for people with horses—it's just a coincidence that the creek the campground is named for is actually *Horse* Creek—and most of the campsites even include a little corral. Nearby are miles and miles of interconnected riding trails through the forests of Sitka spruce, Douglas-fir, and western hemlock. The trails are open to hikers, too, making it by far the most extensive trail network I know of anywhere in Oregon's Coast Range.

We awoke to a chorus of Swainson's thrushes, robins, and varied thrushes. After a short walk to admire the Indian-pipes and *Moneses uniflora* (sometimes called one-flowered wintergreen) blooming in the adjacent forest, we broke camp and drove back down to Highway 101, then north to the northernmost of the three parking lots in Neptune State Park, where Gwynn Creek pours into the sea after passing under the highway in a concrete, fish-friendly culvert. From there, it was little more than a quarter of a mile to our breakfast spot.

Offshore now, small groups of gulls and brown pelicans—but never both species in the same flock—make their way northward against the still-developing north-northwest wind. Occasionally, a harbor seal pokes its head out of the water. Although it's midday and the temperature in the Willamette Valley just fifty miles east of here is likely well into the 80s by now, it's just 61 degrees here and is unlikely to get much warmer, even by late afternoon. The fog, the prevailing north wind, and the cold seawater which wells up at this season just offshore here, combine to keep the air too chilly for much summertime sunbathing along Oregon's coast. The best time to do that is between October and May. Especially during lulls between winter storms, the air is often calm, the daytime temperature in the 60s, and the beach can be quite delightful.

Although the rock just offshore here is very resistant basalt, the headland on which I'm sitting is much softer sedimentary rock, typical of most of the Coast Range. But wherever there are high, steep headlands or promontories along this part of the coast, the rock is Late-Eocene volcanic basalt which was originally overlaid with younger, softer sedimentary rock. The latter eroded off and has left exposed the much more resistant basalt, sometimes in almost horizontal shelves—such as in the area where I had breakfast—and occasionally in haystack-like masses, commonly referred to as sea stacks, just offshore.

The outermost seawater-pounded basalt reefs here are covered with tiny forests of what appear to be palm trees, maybe a foot high. These are a species of brown kelp (*Postelsia palmaeformis*) actually called sea palms that are incredibly sturdy and can withstand the constant pounding of the Pacific as it reaches land here.

One of the first Europeans to see this part of the Northwest coast was the British explorer Captain James Cook, whose ship *HMS Resolution* arrived offshore here on March 7, 1778. His name remains on this point of land, the ridge just east of here—cloaked with enormous Sitka spruces and called Captain Cook Ridge—and a narrow, deep chasm just north of where I'm sitting, called Cook's Chasm, which is spanned at its upper end by an attractive, recently reconstructed bridge of Oregon's coast highway.

The woody vegetation here includes salal, coyote-brush, and Sitka spruce, all of which are severely pruned by the salty mist carried on the summertime northwest winds. The mist is deposited on the windward side of the plants and releases its salt when it dries. The salt then sucks the water out of leaves, twigs, and other tissues on that part of the plant that is most exposed, resulting in plants that truly look as if they have been sheared because the branches on the plants' north sides are stunted or dead, while branches on the south or leeward sides of the plants develop normally.

Although the wind gusts of *winter* storms here on the coast are stronger than the daily summertime winds, the wind almost always comes from the southwest and is accompanied by heavy rain—which washes off any salt that otherwise might accumulate on the southwest sides of plants—so this shearing effect does not occur at that season. But the diurnal northwest *summer* winds here blow nearly every day, especially in the afternoon and into the evening, and are clearly capable of affecting the appearance of seaside vegetation.

The headland behind me, to the east, is forest covered these days, and the canopy is composed almost entirely of Sitka spruce. But when Captain Cook first saw this headland that now bears his name, it looked very different. It was at that time a mostly treeless grassland that had been created and maintained through the millennia by area aborigines who lived much of the year in partly subterranean plank houses along coastal estuaries, where their villages were more protected from winter storms than they would have been on the open coastline.

During the summer, the local people moved north and south along the coast both in search of food and for trade with other tribes. Movement was easy along level parts of the coast dominated by beach and actively moving sand dunes. But where there were headlands, the people were forced to go up and over the headland. To walk through dense coastal forest would have been a challenge—and keeping a trail open and passable where undergrowth is as rank as it often is here would have been difficult. It was evidently much easier to just set fire to the headland, as needed, to keep trees out and maintain a grassland. In the absence of Indian-set fires over the past century, however, forest has reclaimed most of Lane County's former coastal grasslands.

Although the sea level has remained constant for about the past 6,000 years—following the melting of continental glaciers at the end of the most recent Ice Age—Lane County's shoreline has changed since then due to erosion, as well as from uplifting or subsidence due to earthquakes and other tectonic forces. The coastline will of course continue to change. And if the planet's average temperature continues to increase and more polar ice melts, as currently predicted, the sea level will surely rise and likely submerge some of the landscape I see here today.

When I was ready to return to the car, I decided to walk just up the hill behind me to the coast highway, which was little more than 100 feet away, rather than follow the basalt shelf back to Gwynn Creek, the way I'd come earlier in the day. I wanted to see just how close I'd come to being at the northwest corner of Lane County, as I anticipated a sign along the highway to indicate the county line. Indeed, as I climbed over the guardrail at the top of the hill, I noticed not fifty feet to the north a green sign with white lettering: WELCOME TO LINCOLN COUNTY—HEART OF THE OREGON COAST.

I'm confident that, just on the other side was a sign greeting *south*bound travelers that said "Welcome to Lane County," and I was tempted to go see. But then I reminded myself that peeking around to look at the sign's north side would violate my premise of staying within the boundaries of Lane County this year, as it would require that at least part of my body leave Lane County to see the sign! So I turned my back on the sign and returned to the car in the parking lot by Gwynn Creek Knoll—actually an old Indian midden—while enjoying the view of the Pacific from the west side of the highway.

LANE COUNTY'S SOUTHWEST CORNER

My friend Robin and I spent the night along Forest Road 24 northeast of Canary, where it was absolutely silent until daybreak, at which time the dawn chorus began, consisting mostly of singing Swainson's thrushes and another species of thrush called a varied thrush. Late in the night, the fog had moved in from the coast and began condensing on the trees, then dripping to the ground and onto our tents. It was such a pleasant sound—so gentle—that I just lay in my tent and enjoyed it. I knew it wasn't rain and I knew it would likely cease before it was time to get up. Indeed, when I finally sat up in my tent to get dressed, it was quiet again, except for the occasional Pacific slope flycatcher or Swainson's thrush.

We broke camp and headed back down out of the hills toward Highway 101, then turned south and passed Dunes City. After crossing the outlet of Siltcoos Lake, called the Siltcoos River, we drove toward the beach and parked at the trailhead for the Waxmyrtle Trail. The trail led west along the south side of the Siltcoos River estuary before turning southwest to skirt a marsh and eventually arrive at the beach.

Just before reaching the beach, we elected to have breakfast on the west side of the marsh. During our one-hour stay, we were visited by a great blue heron, several killdeer, and several small flocks of cedar waxwings. After the breakfast dishes were done and everything was packed up again, we proceeded along the trail and up and over the foredune, where we got our first good view of the Pacific. I broke into a smile, as it's been years—I'm sorry to say—since I've visited an Oregon beach. But I was smiling particularly because right in front of us, scurrying along the edge of the incoming surf, was a flock of more than a hundred sanderlings. These tiny shorebirds are one of my favorites, as they tirelessly follow advancing wavelets and receding wavelets, probing the sand with their short bills, then flying off together to the next suitable feeding spot fifty or a hundred feet away.

From where we arrived at the beach, it was less than half a mile's walk to reach the southwest corner of Lane County. I don't own or carry a GPS device, as I have no need for one. It was enough to know that I was really close to the corner—certainly within a few hundred feet. Visitors here are restricted to the "wet sand" area of the beach, as the dry sand and driftwood area a little higher on the beach is prime nesting habitat for the endangered snowy plover, a relative of both sanderlings and killdeer. Humans aren't permitted in that area, at the base of the foredune, from March 15 through September 15, and dogs and vehicles are completely banned from this stretch of Oregon's coast.

A mile or so away, however, just to the north of the Siltcoos River, it's another story, as motorized vehicles are permitted in that area. Even where we had our breakfast, we could occasionally hear their engines in the distance. I appreciate having places on public land along the Oregon coast where such vehicles are forbidden. But I would prefer that they be forbidden everywhere. It's not that they're particularly destructive, as they are generally confined to areas of open sand. For me, it's the noise. I just don't agree with the idea that everyone and all their diverse interests must be accommodated on public land—especially when some of those interests conflict with the interests of those of us who are using the public land in a more light-handed way.

But back to my little corner of the county here, and the view I have to the west, from where I'm sitting on the beach. Ahead of me lies the pacific Pacific—at least today, in mid-summer. The tide is going out; the sanderlings are apparently enjoying themselves and filling their tummies; and I'm relieved to see no fishing boats, no off-shore wind turbines, and simply no signs of humanity. It's important to me to know that places like this exist, even if I seldom visit them.

To the south and north—my left and right—the beach appears to go on without end until it disappears into the coastal mist. For a while, a white U.S. Forest Service pick-up stood poised for action to the north, where the Waxmyrtle Trail meets the beach. Not long after I'd chosen this spot and pulled out my sit-upon to sit upon, and my clipboard to write on, the pick-up headed in this direction, probably to monitor activity on this part of the beach and ensure that the few people who are here are keeping out of snowy plover habitat. The population of these small, mostly white shorebirds has become so precarious due both to natural changes in their habitat as well as human intrusions, that I'm willing to accept this level of monitoring.

To my east—that is, behind me—is a relatively new arrival upon the Oregon coast scene. It's called a *foredune*, and has developed at the top of the beach only in the past century, following the introduction of European beach grass. Before EBG took root here, sand annually moved onto the beach from the ocean, and was transported farther inland by the wind. As the dunes swept inland, they were constantly fed by new sand arriving from the ocean. But since the foredune has arisen, it's created a barrier to the arrival of new sand. The active dunes continue to move eastward, but once the blowing sand is removed down to the water table at the western base of the ever-advancing dunes, plants move into the area, from marsh plants to shore pines, and the area is quickly transformed into forest. The marsh by which we had breakfast did not exist fifty years ago. Only since the development of the foredune has the sand that initially covered that area been blown inland, exposing the water table and forming a marsh.

This is not a bad thing in the short run, as rich new habitats—from marshland to forest—continue to arise where once there was only blowing sand. But in the long run, it's unclear what will happen to the areas of actively moving dunes which, as barren as they appear, are themselves an important habitat. If the actively moving dunes were to disappear, they would likely take with them a host of plants and animals that are dependent on them.

Back here on the beach, the high tide line is strewn with countless desiccated bodies of by-the-wind-sailors, a bluish jellyfish relative that floats on the ocean surface and has a transparent "sail" rising vertically from the little animal's body. As their name suggests, they are at the mercy of the wind and when the wind blows them landward and they end up on the beach sand, they soon succumb. The beach here is littered with millions of them. Before sitting down here, I carefully positioned myself *upwind* of them, as downwind there is a bit of a stench.

While I was writing here, a passing jogger stopped to say hello. I recognized his German accent, and he said that he and his wife have been coming to this spot every summer for eight years now. Most years, they've stayed at nearby Waxmyrtle Campground for two to three weeks. (German workers are rewarded with very generous paid vacations.) This year, they're staying for four weeks. I praised him for staying in one spot and getting to know one area very well, instead of many places only slightly, as most visitors do.

He said that they favor this part of the coast because, thanks to the snowy plovers and the extensive areas that are off-limits to human access, very few people come here. He and a jogging woman—not his wife—are the only other people I've seen here, besides the Forest Service pick-up truck driver, during the entire two hours or so that I've been here on this pleasant summer day. He also feels that, by using the campground that is sadly very little used otherwise, especially during the week, they're helping at least a little to ensure that it is not closed due to lack of use.

Well, it's time for a swim, or at least a dip. As I said, it's been so many years since I've been at an Oregon beach, it would be a shame to leave again without having enjoyed the water. So here I go!

While speaking with the German visitor, he asked me if I were "watching the waves"—or at least that's what I understood him to have said. I thought that maybe he was gently suggesting to me that, from time to time, I should look up from my writing and observe my surroundings. I answered, "Oh, yes, aren't the waves beautiful?" "No, not the waves, the *whales!*" Here, he had seen whales spouting just offshore, so after stripping off my clothes and wading into the surf, I kept my eyes open.

And sure enough, less than a quarter-mile from the beach, I saw the spouts and occasionally the backs of five gray whales, including one calf, as they surfaced after feeding. Then, not a minute later, I spotted a harbor seal less than fifty feet away from me who was curious, I suppose, to see a naked and blubber-less human being in such cold water. Indeed, I'd been sternly reminded, the moment I stepped into the water, that there's a reason few people go into the water off Oregon's coast. (I later checked the temperature of the water with my field thermometer and it was 53 degrees, which is coincidentally the *warmest* temperature the McKenzie River ever reaches in summer near McKenzie Bridge, Oregon, where I go for a very quick dip almost every week.)

But the sun was shining, the water was crystal-clear, and there was very little wind, so I continued on out through the foaming surf to where the comparatively small waves were just beginning to break. I waited for just the right one and then I launched myself beachward and slid along the face of the wave as it broke just behind me and carried me along with it. The ride was a short one, but it was a ride! I went back into deeper water several more times to ride more waves, before returning to the beach to replace the body heat I'd lost during less than ten minutes in that cold water.

I was one happy guy, having been able to celebrate my first visit to the beach in years—and my first visit to Lane County's southwest corner—by bodysurfing on such an isolated stretch of the coast, and all the time within view of both gray whales and a harbor seal.

MY ASCENT OF EL POPO

Some years ago, when looking at a map of the Siuslaw (sigh-OO-slaw) National Forest—located in the western part of Oregon's Coast Range, and stretching from south of Florence nearly to Tillamook—I came across a mountain peak with a most unusual name. Although nearby peaks had English names such as Goodwin Peak and Mount Grayback, what piqued my interest was one name of apparently Aztec origin. Although Lane County has plenty of American Indian place names such as Siltcoos Lake and Willamette (once Wallamut) River, this clearly Mesoamerican name is unique.

It wasn't until this year that I finally had the opportunity to visit Mount Popocatépetl (poh-poh-kah-TAY-peh-tull). In a mountain range of very few remarkable peaks, this one is especially unremarkable. At just under one thousand feet in elevation, it is barely distinguishable among the nearby ridges and peaks, many of which are between 800 and 1,200 feet high. And yet sometime in the past, it was given a most impressive name.

Lewis McArthur, in *Oregon Geographic Names*, claims that "the peak was named about 1888 by R. O. Collier, a government surveyor, because it was so hard to climb. The crew was smoking hot when it reached the top." McArthur also claims that Mount Popocatépetl is "a well-known point in the Oregon Coast Range." But in anticipation of my visit, I asked dozens of Lane County residents about this peak, and not a single person had ever heard of it. So I'm not quite sure what to believe.

At any rate, the "other" Mount Popocatépetl is in Mexico. It is an active volcano and is the second highest peak in the country. Its name is said to come from the Nahuatl (or Aztec) words *popoca* ("it smokes") and *tepetl* ("mountain"), or Smoking Mountain. These days, it is popularly referred to as El Popo, and is apparently relatively easy to climb—except, of course, during occasional periods of volcanic activity—despite its *very* remarkable summit elevation of nearly 18,000 feet.

My own ascent of Lane County's El Popo was not particularly eventful, but neither was it easy. My friend Robin and I approached the peak from the west via Forest Road 4830, having left the coast highway at Honeyman State Park and then followed a county road via Canary to the turnoff onto the 4830. Even with a good topographic map, it was difficult to tell where the peak was, but eventually we arrived at what I'm confident was the right place. The peak is near the northeast corner of Section 23, Township 19 South, Range 11 West, and as the tiny gravel forest road makes its way eastward, it tightly hugs the peak's steep north slope.

From where we parked the car, the summit couldn't have been more than 100 yards away, yet there was no way to ascend directly from the north, as a steep cutbank precluded access. So we walked east along the road until we reached an east-west ridge that led up to the summit somewhat more gently. Robin soon decided that even that route to the top, through thickets of salmonberry and evergreen huckleberry, and over and under fallen trees, was beyond her ability, so she returned to the car to have her lunch.

But I was a man on a mission, and that mission was to scale Lane County's own El Popo and eat my picnic lunch at the summit. So I crashed onward and upward through the at times forbidding understory, letting out more than a few yips and groans as I surmounted one after another of the obstacles in my path. Only fifteen or twenty minutes after I'd left the road, I stood on the broad, wooded summit of Mount Popocatépetl. Although I can't claim to have been "smoking hot" upon reaching the top, I was a little sweaty and very much relieved to have made it.

As I sat at the base of a large Douglas-fir to eat my lunch—a plain white bagel with butter and cheddar cheese and mustard, followed by a cookie—I thought of what the peak must have looked like when first climbed by Euro-Americans in the 1880s. To this day, the summit has never been logged, and yet the trees growing there aren't very old. That's because extensive forest fires swept much of the Coast Range during the mid-1800s, killing the preceding stands of trees on Mount Popocatépetl and allowing new Douglas-firs to seed in from the few post-fire survivors scattered throughout the area. So the view the survey crew had in 1888 was very different from my own, as the trees back then would have been only thirty to forty years old. Had the crew in fact arrived thirty or forty years earlier, they might have indeed seen El Popo smoking. But it would have been smoking due to a forest fire, and not because it was an erupting volcano.

Besides my smacking lips enjoying a late and well-earned lunch, I heard very few sounds during my visit to the summit. A nearby Swainson's thrush occasionally burst into song, and several times I heard the coo-cooing of band-tailed pigeons high in the canopy. Thankfully, the Coast Range is spared the annoying and incessant noise of commercial jets flying overhead that disturbs the tranquility of the Cascade Range to the east, which lies beneath a major north-south flight corridor.

I'm not yet finished climbing Lane County's peaks of "foreign" origin. Later this year, at the other end of the county, I plan to ascend Fuji Mountain. I can't wait to announce to my friends that in 2014 I scaled both Mount Popocatépetl and Fuji Mountain without ever leaving the county.

LANE COUNTY'S TWO SUMMERTIME FACES

As part of my birthday celebration the second week of July, I joined my friend Robin for three days in western Lane County, both along the coast itself as well as somewhat inland in the forests of the Coast Range. We avoided the main highways as much as possible, and followed instead the quiet and little-used forest roads in the Siuslaw National Forest.

On our way to the coast from Eugene, for example, after reaching Mapleton, we turned north on Highway 36 toward Deadwood—instead of south and west along Highway 126 to Florence. At Shoemaker Creek, we ascended the North Fork Siuslaw Road which carried us up and over a forested ridge, then down past McLeod Creek and an old "pioneer trail," and over to the site of Minerva, which a century ago had a post office, but today no longer exists.

We then turned north up the Upper North Fork Siuslaw Road toward a site known as Pawn. From there, we ascended a second ridge, after which we made our way down to the Pacific Ocean (and Highway 101) on Cape Creek Road, which disgorges its visitors near the Heceta Head Lighthouse, just north of the Cape Creek Tunnel.

Likewise, on our trip back to Eugene, we again avoided busy Highway 126 between Florence and Mapleton, and instead went east from Honeyman State Park, past Woahink Lake and Canary, and then up into the Coast Range on Forest Road 4830. Later in the day, after visiting Lane County's own Mount Popocatépetl, we turned north and entered the Sweet Creek watershed, which took us back down to the Siuslaw River and Mapleton.

For three days, while the Willamette Valley baked in 90-plus-degree heat under clear skies, we had been blessed at the coast with temperatures in the low- to mid-60s, with cloudy or foggy skies much of the time, but interspersed with sunny breaks. Indeed, when we arrived in Mapleton at 6 p.m. on the last leg of our trip, the temperature was still just 63 degrees. Although the sun was shining, we could see a bank of low clouds just to the west, and an eastbound sea breeze was blowing.

Like many Lane County residents, I've long been aware of the county's two different summertime faces—when the coast feels all day long like a refrigerator and inland areas feel like a furnace—but I thought it would be fun to track the temperature as we drove eastward from Mapleton to Eugene that evening. Every five minutes or so, then, I noted our location as well as the outside temperature displayed just below the odometer on the car's dashboard.

And here's what I found:

Time	Location	Temperature
6:08 pm	Mapleton	63°
6:13	Hwy 126 tunnel	68°
6:20	Austa	71°
6:27	Walton	73°
6:33	Broad open valley west of Noti	75°
6:36	Poodle Creek Road	78°
6:42	Veneta stop light	83°
6:47	Fern Ridge Reservoir	86°
6:51	Greenhill Road	87°
6:57	Bailey Hill Road	88°
7:02	18th & Polk in Eugene	92°

From Mapleton to Fern Ridge Reservoir, we were accompanied by the strong sea breeze which late in the day brings cooler air inland from the coast. But once we were past Fern Ridge, the breeze dissipated and switched to the usual diurnal north wind that blows in the southern Willamette Valley in the summer. Indeed, this wind is what keeps Eugene's summer weather tolerable on especially hot days, and it usually blows continuously from late forenoon until evening. Occasionally, however, it's replaced in the evening by the sea breeze from the west; but most days, that's not the case, and the sea breeze dies out just past Veneta.

On the other hand, the city of Corvallis—which lies just forty miles north-northwest of Eugene—benefits from the cooling sea breeze almost every day during the summer, as the city lies right at the foot of the Coast Range, rather than well out into the Willamette Valley as Eugene does.

Because I don't own a motorized vehicle, I rarely get to the coast, as there is no public transit between Eugene and Florence, and only one infrequent and relatively expensive privately owned bus. Instead, I go to the Cascades on a regular basis, as on weekdays there are four buses daily, in each direction, between Eugene and McKenzie Bridge. So it was a real treat to spend three wonderful days in Lane County's refrigerator. Needless to say, it was a shock to open the car door just one hour's drive from refrigerated Mapleton, and be blasted by the oven-like air which even at 7 p.m. still hung over Eugene.

And I reminded myself that, just as my own refrigerator and oven aren't very far apart from each other in my kitchen, Lane County's refrigerator and oven are also very accessible. Want a hot, dry summer day? Spend it in the Willamette Valley or the West Cascades. But if you prefer a cooler and more humid day, all you need to do is get in the car and head for the coast, which is only a little more than an hour away.

FRUITS DU JOUR * — AND A VEGETABLE

I never thought that the checkout clerks in the local grocery stores I visit regularly ever noticed or cared about what items marched past them on the conveyor belt. After all, they must deal with hundreds of customers every day. How could they ever remember who buys what, even if it's a regular customer? And why would they care to?

Then, one day, a checkout clerk asked me if I hadn't inadvertently picked up a carton of *whole* milk instead of my usual two-percent. I didn't know what to say or to think. If she'd noticed *that*, what else was I doing that registered with her and perhaps with other clerks? So I asked her, "You've probably also wondered, then, why I rarely buy fresh fruits or vegetables, hmm?" She acknowledged that, yes, as a matter of fact, she had noticed that, and thought that maybe I went to another store for fresh produce, or perhaps a local year-round farmers market.

So I told her—no one else was in line behind me—that I grow virtually all of the fruits and vegetables I eat, and except for an occasional bunch of bananas in the middle of winter, or a few oranges around Christmas-time, I eat only what I grow. And I eat well, with fresh fruits and vegetables a part of every meal for much of the year, and fruits I've preserved (usually by freezing) in winter and early spring.

In fact, one day when a third-grade class from a nearby elementary school visited my garden, we decided that it would be fun to list everything I grow. And the list astounded even me: 14 kinds of fruits and 28 kinds of vegetables, wow! What's available to eat fresh varies, of course, with the

fruits du jour is pronounced in French "froo-EE doo ZHOOR"

season. In late summer, I'm able to choose among more than a dozen vegetables and half a dozen fruits, but by February, the only fresh fruit I'll have left are some apples, and I might have less than a half-dozen fresh vegetables to choose from in my winter garden.

As rich and varied as my diet at home is, it's much simpler when I come to the woods to spend a few days. Fresh produce is heavy to carry, takes up a lot of space in my pack, and doesn't travel well, especially in the heat of summer. So I usually have dried apples with my oatmeal in the morning, and no fruit or vegetable with my lunch or dinner. I figure that a few days without my usual cornucopia of fruit and vegetable choices won't hurt me—and it hasn't. Then, when I return home, I'll appreciate my garden bounty all the more.

But it's August now, and partly to escape the heat in town—day after beastly hot day this summer in the 90s—I've spent the past three days here in the West Cascades. And I've eaten fresh fruit and a vegetable (singular) every day. For my first and third breakfasts, I had oatmeal—once with dried apples from last year, and once with dried apricots purchased in a store. But on the second morning, when I traditionally have pancakes, I chopped one-third of a fragrant Gravenstein apple into the batter, and oh, were those pancakes extra good. The apple had traveled here with me in its own private compartment, a pint-size cottage-cheese tub, where it lay swaddled in a paper towel to protect it from unanticipated bumps along the way. Following each of my two evening meals, I also ate one-third of the same apple. (Don't want to overdo it on fresh fruit, you know!)

Then I've had three lunches. Dessert for Lunch #1 was fresh strawberries that, like the apple, traveled here in the privacy of their own one-cup plastic yogurt container. They did fine without any padding. Before lunch, I cut them up, sprinkled them with a little sugar, and by dessert time, they were exceedingly delicious.

For my second lunch—which I ate while sitting next to a beautiful spring here on the ridge, where the luscious water arrives above-ground at 49 refreshing degrees Fahrenheit—I extricated a small and just-ripe peach from its little yogurt container. Like the apple, it had been protected from bumps by a crumpled paper towel. With the large blade of my sharp-as-a-razor Swiss Army pocket knife, I gently cut off a slice at a time, then carefully wrapped my lips around it and, with closed eyes, savored slice after slice until it was finished.

Just a bit ago, Lunch #3 concluded with what I consider to be a fruit of the gods, or the mango of the temperate zone: a nectarine. This is the first year I've had a really good crop on my tree, as nectarines can be a bit tricky in our climate because they bloom so early and often get hit by frost. But this was a lucky year, and my small tree produced around 150 nectarines. Only one of them was selected to accompany me to the woods and, as it wouldn't be eaten until the third day, I chose one which wasn't quite ripe yet.

But today was its day to serve as my lunchtime dessert, and it had ripened just perfectly. Like the peach and the apple, it made the trip in a private compartment (its own one-cup yogurt container) and when I opened the lid, I got a preliminary whiff of the aroma that only a well-ripened nectarine has. Soon, I was once again expertly brandishing my pocket knife, cutting off individual slices and almost drooling over each piece as it headed for my mouth.

Lastly, I brought with me my first European-style cucumber of the season. They grow on a trellis just outside my sunroom, so I can watch them mature at eye-level from inside the house and not let a single one escape my notice as harvest-day approaches. Cukes travel pretty well, but I still rolled this one up in some newspaper and put a rubber band around it, then carried it in an outer pocket of my backpack, where it was least likely to be hurt.

At each lunch, I sliced a plain bagel in two, then buttered the two halves and added sliced cheddar cheese and Plochman's mustard. Atop the mustard—which serves in part to hold the next layer in place—several cucumber slices graced the open-faced sandwich's top, making it picture-perfect with the gold cheddar, the brownish mustard, and the moist white disks of cucumber encircled in thin green peel.

So I haven't been completely deprived of fresh food while here in The Woods. Rather, what produce I did elect to bring along received far more attention—because of its scarcity and the relative difficulty of getting it here—than it ever would have gotten at home. The lives of those four fruits and one vegetable, now over, were good lives right up to the end. And my life here in The Woods has been just a little better because of them.

TWO COMMON MISCONCEPTIONS

More than twenty years ago, I offered a one-day field class through Lane Community College's Continuing Education program entitled Upper Willamette Valley. The class description referred to the day's itinerary by the habitat types we'd visit—forest, savanna, and grassland—during the course of the day, rather than mentioning place names. It wasn't until the morning of the class that I realized the mistake I'd made, as several of the people who'd signed up for the class thought that we were going to the Portland area.

The first thing I had to do, then, was open up a map of Oregon and explain to my students which way the Willamette River flowed—north to Portland from the Eugene-Springfield metropolitan area—and remind everyone that water flows downhill. Then off we went on a loop tour that included Centennial Butte, Indianhead, Twin Buttes, the Pine Grove church along Peoria Road, Irish Bend along the Willamette River, and Kirk Pond north of Fern Ridge Reservoir.

All of those locations are in what has historically been referred to as the Upper Willamette Valley—as opposed to the *Lower* Willamette Valley from, say, the Salem area to Portland. So why do people these days think that from Eugene-Springfield, one goes *up* the valley to Portland?

During the not-so-old days, from the mid-1800s until about the 1950s, people were much more knowledgeable about the landscape they lived in. Early Euro-American settlers in the Upper Willamette Valley were very aware that you rode your horses or drove your wagons *down* the valley to do business in Oregon City. Later, when steamboats plied the Willamette River, it was obvious to travelers that they went *with* the flow of the river

71

down the valley, and *against* the flow on the way back south. They spent more of their lives outside—whether they were farmers or not—and they lived lives that were less sheltered from the elements and the landscape surrounding them than our lives are today. Even young children used to know that one went *down* the valley to Portland. But no more.

These days, we hop in our climate-controlled cars and drive "up" the map to Portland via Interstate 5—be it a real paper map or an image from Google. Along the way, we see the Willamette River only once, when we cross it just south of Wilsonville, and it's not at all evident there which way it's flowing. But frankly, most people don't even notice the river as they speed by.

A good friend who lives in Portland and visits Eugene fairly regularly—and who has a four-year degree from the University of Oregon in geography—always tells me he's thinking of "going down to Eugene" for the weekend. Or he wonders when I'm next "coming up" to Portland. If even someone with a geography degree makes such a gross geographical error, I can hardly hold out much hope for the rest of society. But I want people to know the facts anyway.

A second misconception people in Eugene-Springfield have is that our cities lie due south of Portland. Technically, Lane County's two largest cities lie south and a significant distance *west* of downtown Portland. When you go down the valley to Portland, you're actually going down and due north until about Salem, when the road (or the railroad or the river) swings well to the east. Map-language speakers should properly say, then, that they're going "up-and-over" to Portland—although in fact it's down-and-east-a-ways.

I'm aware of this offset because I'm familiar with the grid system of sections and townships from which all real property here in the Northwest has been measured since the Donation Land Claim Act of 1850. Its base point is in the hills west of downtown Portland at a spot once occupied by the Willamette Stone—where now a small obelisk stands in the tiny Willamette Stone State Heritage Site—from which every point in Oregon and Washington is measured.

The north-south line that goes through the stone is called the Willamette Meridian. The east-west line is called the Baseline. Everywhere in the Northwest lies either east or west of the Willamette Meridian, and either north or south of Baseline. Beginning at the Willamette Stone, square townships measuring six miles on a side—each containing 36 numbered square miles or "sections"—are numbered according to how many townships south or north of the Baseline they are, and how many "ranges" east or west of the Meridian they are. For example, the downtown Eugene post office is located in section 31—the southwesternmost section—of T(ownship) 18 S(outh) R(ange) 3 W(est). That is, it is nearly 108 miles (18 townships X 6 miles per township) south of the Willamette Stone and the Baseline, and almost 18 miles (3 ranges X 6 miles per range) west of the stone and the Willamette Meridian. And because the Willamette Meridian itself is three miles west of downtown Portland, Eugene's post office is almost 21 miles west of Portland!

I know, I know: Who cares? Well, if your GPS device or the Google map you're looking at were off by several miles, you'd be rightly upset and possibly even complain to someone about it. So when someone says Eugene is 110 miles *south* of Portland, I complain, because although Eugene is in fact almost exactly that distance south of the Baseline—which runs through downtown Portland—it is also some 21 miles west of downtown Portland. So it would be more correct to say that Eugene lies south *and west* of downtown Portland.

THE INTRUDER

I live in a small house with a 523-square-foot ground floor and an improved loft where I have my office and my bed. Because the upstairs can get quite warm in summer, I move my bed downstairs every year in late spring and sleep next to a large, square window on the east side of the house. Every evening, as the air outside cools, I open wide a skylight upstairs, as well as the east window, and the cool night air moving gently down the hill east of my house flows through the window and across my face, as the day's accumulation of hot air in the house chimneys out via the skylight. It's a simple and effective system.

My neighborhood is very quiet at night, and I sleep soundly most nights, even though both the window and skylight are open. Occasionally, friends will express concern about my safety because all an intruder would have to do to get into my house on a summer night is to push the screen in, and step up onto the windowsill, which is only a few feet above the brick terrace outside the window. I remind those friends that no intruder in his right mind would enter a house if he can see the house's occupant just a few feet from his entry point. Still, some people shudder at the very thought.

Last night, just before 3 a.m., I was awakened by the faint sound of metal scraping against wood. It wasn't very loud, nor was it continuous, but every fifteen or twenty seconds I'd hear it. Because the grapes on the arbor outside my window are just now beginning to ripen, I suspected that this year, once again, a raccoon had discovered my grapes and was clambering around the arbor looking for just the right bunch. Raccoons can be a nuisance, but I just put up with them and try not to let them disturb my sleep too much. If they persist in making a racket, I simply close the window and turn on a small fan for "white noise."

74

The mysterious sound continued, and as I lay in bed debating whether to get up and shut the window, I was startled beyond words by the sudden crash of the window screen as it hit the floor! In complete darkness, my heart racing, I sat up in bed, uncertain what was happening and where the intruder might be in relation to me. I couldn't turn on a light without getting out of bed, and neither did the intruder carry a light so that I knew where he was.

Only then did I realize that the screen that had been pushed in and crashed to the floor was the one on the *upstairs* skylight—not the one on the window near my bed—and that the intruder was not a two-legged one carrying a flashlight, but likely a *four*-legged and furry one with good night vision.

Suddenly, the animal jumped from the stairway landing beneath the skylight—where it had fallen when the screen gave way under its weight—and landed on top of the down comforter that covered my legs. I know how nasty raccoons can be when provoked, so I was fearful that, in getting up to turn on a light, I might step on or near the creature and risk a bite or worse. But I had no choice: the animal was now in my house and wanted to get out, but couldn't.

I groped for my glasses on the nearby table—where I always put them at night—but didn't find them. Had the critter run across the table too and knocked them off? Finally, I reached the light switch and turned it on to reveal on the hardwood floor, just a few feet away from me, a terrified housecat that had been spending its night quietly exploring the neighborhood rooftops, when it happened to stick its nose under the gaping maw of my skylight, then walked onto the screen covering the large rectangular hole cut for the skylight. It apparently walked around the screen for several minutes until the screen gave way under the cat's weight, and CRASH!! Down came both the screen and the cat onto the stairway landing only feet from my bed.

Well, at least I knew now what had happened. But I still couldn't find my glasses and I had a cat going bonkers all over the room, in an effort to get out of this place the fastest way possible. Finally, I saw my glasses on a bookshelf near the bed—how curious, as I seldom put them there—and grabbed them, put them on, and proceeded to figure out how to get the cat out of my house and back outside.

Despite the cat's difficult circumstances, it was not in attack mode, so I might be able to approach it. As I quickly mulled over my choices, the cat was eyeing the big east window as an escape route. NO! I didn't want it to lunge out through there, destroying an expensive and custom-built screen, so I stooped to grab the cat. Off it went like lightning, and up and onto my bed. I pounced on it as it reached the corner of the bed, but it escaped my grip and got beneath the bed, where it proceeded to meow plaintively.

When the cat finally came out from under the bed, I lunged at it again, catching it by the scruff of the neck. I then carried it to the front door, through which I tossed it most unceremoniously onto the front porch. And that was the end of that, no?

No. I'd used so much adrenalin that I was now fully awake and, no matter what I did, my body wouldn't go back to sleep. As I tossed and turned, a little cough developed. What? After a while, I went to get a dose of Nyquil from the medicine cabinet, both to suppress the cough as well as to help me get back to sleep, which I finally did after maybe an hour more of tossing and turning.

It wasn't until I got up this morning that I figured out the source of my cough. Here, at the head of the bed, my navy flannel sheet was covered with white cat hairs from when I'd pounced on the cat as it was trying to escape. Because I'm mildly allergic to cats, and that part of the sheet was where my head lay after the break-in, my body was simply reacting to the cat hair.

I awoke to a completely quiet neighborhood, and the early morning sunlight was streaming in the east window onto the little vase of black-eyed susans on my table, illuminating their lovely orange petals. The peaceful scene was in such stark contrast to the circus that had taken place only five hours earlier, I just had to smile. Had a cat really fallen through the skylight during the night, or was it just a nightmare I had? The answer to both of those questions is yes: A cat *did* fall through the skylight, and it *was* a nightmare, and one I'll not soon forget.

AUFDERHEIDE DRIVE: A DREAM COME TRUE

As I was zigzagging up the first long, steep hill on Day One of our three-day bicycle trip, I was thinking of at least two reasons why I'd not been on a multi-day bike tour since my two-month-long transcontinental bike trip with my brother, Scot, in 1980: 1) it's hard work; and 2) I'm now 62 years old instead of 28. But putting those thoughts aside, and thinking instead of how good it would feel once I got to the top, I pressed on.

The most difficult part of the day was already past, as I had had to get myself out of bed at the inhumane hour of 3:45 a.m. in order to catch the 4:47 McKenzie Bridge bus at Eugene Station. It's the earliest bus in the entire Lane (County) Transit District system, and most of the half-dozen or so riders headed upriver at that time of day were U. S. Forest Service employees who work at the ranger station just past McKenzie Bridge. But my friend, Nick, and I had decided on the early start to ensure that we could get both our bikes and our two little bike trailers on the bus without any competition from other cyclists, as might have been the case if we had waited for the second bus of the day which left at 8:20.

I'd wanted to do this trip for more than three decades, since I first moved to Eugene in 1983, but somehow, it just never happened. The planets, however, were evidently aligned in just the right position this year for the trip to take place.

The Robert Aufderheide Memorial Drive—which also has the shorter but more boring moniker of Forest Road 19—is a 65-mile-long, two-lane, paved road through the West Cascades that links the McKenzie River valley and Highway 126 with the Middle Fork Willamette River and Highway 58. For most of its length, it's little used, except by Forest Service employees and occasional tourists. Over the course of the three mid-summer days we were on it, we saw fewer than 100 motorized vehicles, and that was just fine with us. (Weekends, however, are likely much busier, which is why we purposely visited mid-week.)

Our first stop after getting off the bus was the spectacular old-growth forest stand at Delta Campground, where the South Fork of the McKenzie meets the main stem of the river. Despite the campground's gorgeous setting and the fact that it was August, the peak of the camping season, there were only two sites taken. Because of the still-early hour—we'd gotten off the bus around 6 a.m.—we rolled absolutely silently through the campground to its far end, where the "nature trail" loop begins and ends. After parking our bikes, we entered The Big Woods. I often take visitors to this stand, especially if their mobility is limited in any way, as it's fully accessible and gives the visitor a splendid taste of centuries-old Douglas-fir/hemlock forests.

Then, before ascending the aforementioned long hill to the breast of the Cougar Reservoir dam, I took Nick to see the fabulous state-of-the-science Fish Collection Facility at the base of the dam, where returning spring chinook salmon ascend a fish ladder into a holding pool, and are then transferred without ever leaving the water into a specially designed truck that carries them above the reservoir, where they're released into the South Fork to continue the journey to the gravel spawning beds where they themselves hatched three to four years earlier. It's an amazing set-up that ensures that the South Fork salmon population can continue to exist despite the presence of a huge flood-control dam.

After our brief visit, we found a quiet spot nearby, next to the river, where we cooked and ate our breakfasts before ascending that first hill. Once we'd reached the top of the dam, we cooled off in the breezy shade of some scrawny, completely out-of-context shore pines (native to Oregon's coast) before continuing around the west side of the reservoir. Although we'd planned to visit the very popular Terwilliger Hot Springs—I hadn't been there since the mid-1980s—we had second thoughts once we arrived at the entrance and saw a half-dozen cars in the parking lot and learned that a $6 per person fee is now charged.

So we continued on to the south end of the reservoir, and another empty campground at Cougar Crossing. Just a few miles upriver from there, we found an idyllic spot to have our lunches and rest a while. I went for a refreshing dip in the pristine water of the South Fork and, after having my lunch, strung up my hammock between two red alder trees—as Nick had done with his own hammock just after our arrival—and proceeded to enjoy the siesta.

We continued pedaling later in the afternoon and set up our first camp in early evening in a magnificent stand of trees about midway between French Pete and Frissell Crossing campgrounds. Another dip in the South Fork, then dinner, and finally to bed under starry skies barely visible through the small breaks in the forest canopy. I slept in my tent, and Nick spent the night in his hammock.

The morning of Day Two, a light mist was falling, so I cooked my mini-pancakes under my tarp lean-to, and by the time we hit the road again mid-morning, the mist had let up. For several miles, the road led through more stands of magnificent trees. Although Nick had bicycled the Aufderheide several years before—and in a single day—the whole idea of taking three days to go the 65 miles was to enjoy stopping along the way as often as we wanted. In particular, I wanted to see what the many campgrounds were like, so we stopped at all of them—as well as at many tributary creeks as we went along.

I knew from studying my topographic maps that Day Two would be the most difficult because of a long, steep climb between Frissell Crossing and Box Canyon, so I was prepared for more zigzagging. Partway up the hill— which follows the rambunctious Roaring River—we stopped near the confluence of McBee Creek and Roaring River and had our lunches on a pleasant little gravel bar by tiny McBee Creek. After lunch, we continued a few hundred yards along the seldom-used Roaring River Ridge trail to an amazingly stout footbridge across the Roaring River. Over time, the bridge's support timbers have softened and rotted, so it tilts downward to one side, but it was still safe to cross. On the other side, we found excellent grazing, with thimbleberries and three species of huckleberries. Below and beside us, the Roaring River lived up to its name as well as its reputation for very cold water, as it issues from large springs not too far away from where we stood. My field thermometer read 43 degrees Fahrenheit—that's mighty cold for a watercourse of that size.

After our postprandial ascent of the rest of the hill, we reached the lovely meadows at the headwaters of McBee Creek, near the Box Canyon Forest Service Guard Station. In the late afternoon light, the asters and owl's clover and grasses of the meadows were especially lovely, and we decided to camp there our second night. Our decision was based in part on the open meadow, where we'd be able to enjoy the starry skies far from the light pollution of the nearest metropolitan areas of Eugene-Springfield and Bend-Redmond-Madras.

We were not disappointed. After making our dinners and waiting for it to get really dark, we exited the stand of Engelmann spruces where we were camped, and were suitably awed by the celestial show arching over the meadow. Neither of us had seen the Milky Way in months—even though we *live* in the Milky Way—and the Summer Triangle (Vega, Altair, and Deneb) was brilliant, as were the other familiar summertime constellations. But eventually, the increasingly cool air temperature persuaded us to retire to our beds for the night.

Day Three dawned with clear skies, and we breakfasted on the west edge of the meadow, not far from the reconstructed Landis Cabin which was first built in the early 1900s by stockmen who used the then much more extensive meadows to graze their sheep or cattle in the summertime.

After breakfast—mine consisted of oatmeal, an egg, a toasted bagel, a pot of tea, and a cookie—came the most difficult part of our trip for me: a mile-long descent into the valley of the North Fork Middle Fork Willamette River (that's its real name!). We would go down nearly one thousand feet in elevation on a thankfully straight road, but I'd have to brake the whole way. The brakes on my 31-year-old twelve-speed Centurion were in good shape, but because of my drop-style ("racing") handlebars, it was very hard on my hands and shoulders to maintain the required pressure and posture for so long a stretch. But I didn't have a choice—unless perhaps I'd wanted to drag a small log behind me. So down I went. When the road started to level out near the bottom, we parked our bikes and took a break by wandering south along the Shale Ridge Trail and into the Waldo Wilderness, designated just thirty years ago this year. We didn't go even a quarter of a mile, but it gave my hands and shoulders the little rest they needed before continuing.

Then, back on the road and past three amusingly named creeks coming into the North Fork from the north side of the road: Minute, Tiny, and Little Creeks. Next stop, Constitution Grove, where a stand of tall Douglas-firs commemorates the signing of the U.S. Constitution in 1787 with a bronze plaque placed in 1987, only a few years after Aufderheide Drive was completed. Attractive wooden plates are attached to a couple of dozen trees in the grove, and each plate includes one signer's name as well as the name of the colony or state he represented.

The road continued downhill all the way to Westfir. Because we had to catch the 4:20 p.m. Diamond Express back to Eugene—a commuter bus running only weekdays that connects workers in the Oakridge-Westfir area with Eugene—we didn't get to dawdle along the way as much as we might have liked to. But we did stop at the U.S. Forest Service's Kiahanie Campground, where we ate our lunches at one of the campsites by the North Fork, and were re-introduced to human beings and barking dogs, in preparation for our return to Eugene and so-called civilization later in the afternoon.

From Kiahanie, then, it was nonstop to Westfir, including a spectacular stretch of road where it switches briefly to the west side of the North Fork as the river plummets down a steep gorge. In Westfir, we had just enough time to get much-deserved ice cream at the little grocery, which we then enjoyed eating at a picnic table at the east end of the Office (or Westfir) Covered Bridge, Lane County's longest. It was only another couple of miles to the Westfir Middle School where we awaited our bus at the park-and-ride there.

What a treat to be able to complete this scenic loop designed for motorists—from Eugene to Blue River to Westfir, and back to Eugene—without having to depend on a privately-owned motor vehicle. The bus from Eugene was free, as both of us have University of Oregon passes, and the Diamond Express back cost only $2.50 each. Although we saw a few other bicyclists during our three days, none of them appeared equipped to be camping along the Aufderheide corridor. Granted, we purposely planned our trip to be in the middle of the week, but I still got the impression that very few people do what we did by completing the entire loop without a car, and stretching it out over several days.

The Aufderheide is just one more amenity here in Lane County that is incredibly accessible to residents, yet it is apparently little used except for the north end access to Terwilliger Hot Springs, and the south end access to several popular swimming holes along the lower North Fork during the summer. I hope to return to Aufderheide Drive again soon—perhaps in mid-October when the fall colors of the abundant vine maples and bigleaf maples along the route will be at their peak.

AN INTERRUPTED NAP

The day before my weekly trip into the woods of the West Cascades, there had been an afternoon thundershower in the mountains. But I was unaware of that because in Eugene—where I live, some sixty miles away—it had been dry all day. So I was completely unprepared to walk through soaking wet forest floor vegetation. All I had were my hiking boots, which aren't especially waterproof. (I seldom carry my rubber boots or my waterproof over-pants during Oregon's long summer drought.)

No matter. By carefully choosing my route through the forest and my individual footsteps, I made it mostly dry-footed to a favorite spot, then set up my green tarp lean-to to spend a quiet day in that one place instead of wandering about and getting both wet shoes and soaked pant legs.

I had a feeling there might be another shower in the clouds overhead, and sure enough, late forenoon, it did rain a bit. I'd eaten my breakfast mid-morning, then had a little nap, did some writing, and the rest of the time just looked out into the forest—four of my favorite activities (eating, sleeping, writing, and daydreaming). And soon it was lunchtime.

After lunch, I lay down again on my wool blanket for another nap. (What a life!) When I'm napping in the woods, I usually lie on my side with my head on a makeshift pillow of whatever extra clothing I have in my pack, and my legs and shoeless feet pulled up slightly toward my torso. It's very comfortable, and both before I fall asleep and as I wake up, I find myself just looking out into the forest.

I'd been sound asleep for maybe an hour—I don't wear a watch when I'm in the woods—when I was gently awakened by the sound of a large animal nearby that was moving slowly through the forest floor vegetation. I know what a deer's movement sounds like, and it wasn't a deer. And there weren't many other choices. I wasn't afraid either, as I've learned through the years that there are really no animals in these woods that I need to fear, as long as I'm prudent in my own actions. And since I was lying on the ground, with my back to the vertical side of my tarp lean-to, and looking out, I knew that I was safe and sound.

So, while still lying down, I opened my eyes. All I saw was greenery. My lean-to is at the base of a bowl-like topographic feature I call Amphitheater, because the nearby hillside rises gently from where I sit or lie, in a 180-degree arc up to a little ridge. And my "audience" is all of the ferns and shrubs looking down on me. There are very few trees on the hillside, so the view is quite open, which I like, as denser forests sometimes make me feel a bit claustrophobic.

Then I noticed some movement toward the top of the slope, maybe fifty or sixty feet away—just some shrubbery shaking in the still air. And shortly after that, I saw the pointed black head of a bear appear. I smiled and said to myself, "Number Six." Because I see bears (and cougars) so seldom, I remember very well each and every one of my encounters with them, and I'd already had five encounters with bears over my thirty years in the woods here.

This bear looked like a yearling—the third I've seen up here—that probably got kicked out of the house fairly recently by its mom, and was just getting accustomed to life on its own. It would have been born early in 2013, so was just over a year old.

I finally sat up slowly to get a better look, but as I did, the bear ambled out of my view and deeper into the forest. It had never caught wind of me, as the air was completely still at the time.

I lay back down, smiling, content to have had another brief encounter with one of the splendid creatures who share this forested ridge with me.

CELEBRATION

I've used my three favorite modes of transportation—bus, bike, and hiking boots—to arrive at this madrone-studded bluff above Separation Creek with a grand view of all Three Sisters peaks, nearly devoid of snow already due to a thin snowpack last winter and then an unusually warm summer. In the foreground are many square miles of unbroken forest, where one is unlikely to find another human being. There are no roads, no machines, no buildings, and no power lines because this is the Three Sisters Wilderness. And I've come here today to celebrate its birthday.

Fifty years ago today, on 3 September 1964, President Lyndon B. Johnson signed the Wilderness Act, which created the National Wilderness Preservation System and protected 9.1 million acres of national forest in wilderness areas. The areas initially designated as wilderness included the bulk of what is called Three Sisters Wilderness in the central Oregon Cascades. But in 1978, the French Pete Addition west of the original wilderness increased its total area significantly. And in 1984, another small chunk was added: this area north of Separation Creek and Rainbow Falls that includes the bluff on which I'm now sitting. It's possible, moreover, that I played a small role in getting this additional area designated as wilderness.

I moved to Eugene from Madison, Wisconsin in late June 1983, and soon began to go on hikes with the Obsidians hiking group. It was through my friend, Anne—whom I'd met on one of the hikes—that I heard about a small group of wilderness advocates who would be accompanying a Eugene television-station crew to this area on 31 July 1983, just a month after my arrival in Eugene. The objective of the group was to bring public attention to this small roadless area that risked being logged someday if it were not included in the adjacent Three Sisters Wilderness, and to show that its inclusion would also help to protect the scenic views from the Rainbow Falls viewpoint at the end of the trail.

As we ascended Foley Ridge on our way to the trailhead that summer morning, we passed many areas that had been logged in just the preceding decade, so it seemed like only a matter of time before this area, too, would be cleared of its trees. Once we reached the viewpoint, the group's leader announced that we would be descending into the U-shaped Separation Creek canyon—where only 15,000 years ago there was a tongue of glacial ice that had oozed down the creek valley from the High Cascades ice sheet just to the east.

I was delighted by the idea, but my enthusiasm was not shared by the young men and women of the TV crew, who were not wearing hiking boots. They were especially reluctant to hike to the bottom of the canyon with all of their equipment. So I offered to carry one of the cameras, someone else carried an equipment case, another person hoisted a big tripod onto his shoulder, and soon we were headed down the steep slope. The crew got some great film footage, including video of me joyfully thrashing about in the frigid whitewater at the base of Rainbow Falls just before it joins Separation Creek.

It was a fun day in the woods for everyone—even the TV crew, it turned out—and a couple of days later, the piece appeared on the news. Less than a year after that, these moss-covered boulders among which I'm now sitting became part of the Three Sisters Wilderness.

Another reason that today is special is that it's my 999th day spent "upriver" since the summer of 1983—yes, I've kept track. My first day was the day just *before* I came up here with the TV crew, when I bicycled from Eugene to Delta Campground near Rainbow—almost fifty miles one-way—and back to Eugene. Throughout the 1980s, I continued to visit the area a half-dozen times each year, on average, and usually brought my bike along on the bus.

But after a bicycle accident in September 1990—when I couldn't ride for several months—I found that I enjoyed exploring the area on foot far more than I had when encumbered by a bicycle. During the 1990s, then, my upriver visits ballooned from 17 days a year in 1991 to as many as 37 in the late 90s. And since 2000, I've averaged 46 days per years, with a high of 60 in 2011.

Besides being my 999th day upriver since 1983, today is my 50th day upriver so far this calendar year, and it looks like I'll reach 75 days total for the year by the end of December. One of the reasons for this year's high number of visits is that, along with my decision to stay within the borders of Lane County for the entire calendar year, I have also elected to camp overnight upriver at least two consecutive nights each month. That's been my aim for many years, but the most overnights in any one year so far was seventeen in 2011. If I hit 24 this year—that is, at least two nights every calendar month—I will have finally achieved my goal.

My first visit to this exact spot was in March 1991, and by early June of that year, I'd come here several more times, including one overnight trip. I thought this was somewhere I'd come on a regular basis, so I left a notebook inside a waterproof plastic sack under one of the boulders here, anticipating writing a few notes in it at every visit. But for some reason— likely my increasing preference for exploring by foot instead of by bike, as I mentioned above—it was several years before my next visit, by which time a rodent had gotten into the sack and nibbled at a few of the journal's pages. So I took it home and never used it again.

My most recent visit to this bluff was in late March 2007—more than seven years ago. Yet today, as I set out to hike the mile-long trail in, I felt as if that visit could have been only weeks or months ago. Nothing has changed very much in those seven years except me, and I had no trouble at all finding this site, which is a short distance away from the trail. It's amazing what one's mind can remember sometimes.

Now, late afternoon, it's finally time to string up my hammock between two madrone tree trunks and take a little nap before returning to the trailhead and biking back downhill to the highway. It took me about two hours to get here—from 1,500 to over 3,000 feet elevation—and, once I get back to my bike, I'll zoom the six-and-a-half miles back downhill in just over fifteen minutes. I'll be smiling all the way, not just to be coasting back downhill, but because I got to celebrate the Wilderness Act's anniversary at one of my favorite places on the planet.

LANE COUNTY'S SOUTHEAST CORNER

I have invited eight good friends to join me in visiting the corner of Lane County that lies just south of Diamond Peak, an area of the county I haven't visited for over two decades. We've come here via Oakridge and the nicely paved Forest Road 21 that skirts the west side of Hills Creek Reservoir, then continues south along the Middle Fork Willamette River before finally turning east. We then turned off onto the well-graded 2154 gravel road which ascends toward Emigrant Pass and Summit Lake.

Along the way, we stopped at Big Pine Opening where, on a south-facing hillside, enormous ponderosa pines raise their lofty canopies above a landscape of grass and wildflowers—most of which are dry and golden or brown now in early September. A number of these natural "openings" occur in this part of the Willamette National Forest, which is otherwise covered with a closed-canopy forest of Douglas-firs. In the absence of the fires that in the past were started by lightning or by the area's aborigines, these areas of scattered trees and grasslands have diminished in extent considerably, as the surrounding Douglas-fir forest has encroached on them.

But at Big Pine Opening, the Forest Service recently removed most of the younger, encroaching trees and used prescribed fire to restore a sizable chunk of grassland—which is important habitat for many sun-loving species of plants, birds, insects, and other animals whose numbers have decreased in proportion to the disappearance of their preferred habitat. In an era when criticism, much of it unwarranted, is still leveled at the Forest Service with regard to timber cutting, in particular, it's heartening to see such thoughtful and ecologically important restoration work on the part of the agency.

After our mid-forenoon snack in the shade of several of the 300-year-old pines, we continued along the Middle Fork to Beaver Creek at about 3,500 feet elevation, where we turned onto the 2154 road and climbed steeply toward the county's corner here at nearly 5,700 feet. About a mile before reaching our goal and the crest of the Cascades—which separates Lane County from Klamath County to the east—I needed to obtain a limited-entry permit from the Douglas County Board of Commissioners so I could briefly enter Douglas County for less than half a mile, where the 2154 road dips to the south before re-entering Lane County and continuing on to Lane's southeast corner. Because I was unable to contact any of the commissioners just then (I had no phone with me), permission was granted instead by the unanimous vote of my fellow adventurers, and we summarily sneaked past the border guards and quickly continued eastward until we were back in Lane County. Whew! Shortly thereafter, the Klamath County sign loomed ahead of us. We had arrived.

Once out of our vehicle, we walked only a couple of hundred yards to Lane County's southeast corner, where we're sitting in an open stand of young (less than 100 years old) lodgepole pines and mountain hemlocks, along with a few western white pines and subalpine firs. The ground is open in most places and covered with pieces of whitish pumice that are noticeably larger than those which we see around our campsite near Waldo Lake. That's because this area is only 32 miles from the former Mount Mazama— the volcano which 7,700 years ago erupted and then collapsed, forming the caldera we call Crater Lake—while our campsite is 48 miles from Mazama, or half again as far. The farther one gets from the volcano, the finer the pumice one finds, as the largest and heaviest pieces fell to the ground closest to the volcano.

Here and there, grouse huckleberry sports its tiny green leaves on plants that are scarcely six inches tall. Elsewhere, dead conifer branches lie on the ground—where they've been bleached by the sun—along with mountain hemlock seed cones. There are a few inexplicable stumps, as well, which were clearly sawed off a long time ago, but why? This area has never been logged, as far as I can tell. It's a mystery.

Even though we're at nearly 6,000 feet, the temperature midday is 76 degrees, which means the Willamette Valley at only a few hundred feet above sea level must be having yet another blistering hot day. There's also a slight smell of wood smoke in the air here, as smoke from the Deception Creek forest fire near Oakridge has drifted this way.

At this season, there are few insects around—just a pesky fly, and someone saw a mosquito (a *single* mosquito!). We purposely didn't come here in July, as this area is notorious for mosquitoes in midsummer. (In fact, it's only a little over two miles to a small body of water west-northwest of here with the uninviting name of Mosquito Lake.) Other than the sound of the fly, it's intensely and refreshingly quiet here. The only other sounds we've heard since our arrival are a red-breasted nuthatch's nasal *neep-neep*, a commercial jet, and a cargo plane.

This area is probably best known historically for the Lost Wagon Train of 1853 which made its way through what is now called Emigrant Pass, only a mile and a half north of here. The wagons were on their way to Oakridge and the Willamette Valley, and locals eventually found the group and guided them there, so no lives were lost.

Interestingly, because the Cascade Crest separating Oregon's west-side counties from the east-side ones is the same line as that which divides watersheds, it is naturally very sinuous in many places. So the southeast tip of Lane County ends up being shaped like a sort of tiny "toe" less than a quarter of a mile from north to south, with Klamath County both north and east of the toe, and Douglas County to the south.

Although the ground is dry at this season, this area is snow-covered most years from sometime in November until well into June or even July some years. Based on the "lichen lines" on trees in the vicinity—lichens on the trees' trunks survive only above the winter snowpack—the average maximum snowpack here is about six feet.

This corner of Lane County is by far the most remote of the four. The northwest corner is just feet from Highway 101; the southwest corner is only a couple of miles from the same busy highway. And the northeast corner is a few hundred yards from Highway 242 at McKenzie Pass. During the course of our visit here, only one or two vehicles have passed, and it's Sunday, the biggest day of the week for recreationists here in the High Cascades. Imagine how few people pass through this area on a weekday.

I'd love to visit nearby Summit Lake again, as we're so close; the only other time I was there was in the 1980s. But the Klamath County border guards are notoriously touchy about visitors like myself who don't have formal permission to enter their county, so in a little while, we'll be heading back down the Middle Fork, and then returning to our campsite at Waldo Lake. It's been a pleasure visiting this very little known corner of Lane County, and I look forward to coming back again someday, maybe in winter and on cross-country skis.

LANE COUNTY'S NORTHEAST CORNER

Most of the central Oregon Cascades were still hazy yesterday from lingering forest fires and a lack of air movement, but later in the day a fresh air mass arrived from the Pacific and today the air is crystal clear—at least here in the mountains. My friends and I left our camp near Waldo Lake mid-forenoon and proceeded west on Highway 58 to Oakridge and Westfir, where we then followed the Aufderheide Memorial Drive through the West Cascades to the McKenzie Valley.

After a picnic lunch at peaceful Limberlost Campground along the Old McKenzie Highway (Highway 242)—and a refreshing drink for me straight out of pristine Lost Creek—we headed up the switchbacks of Dead Horse Grade to the High Cascades plateau and then skirted the south edge of a lava flow that occurred only about 3,000 years ago. Shortly after Craig Lake, as we were approaching McKenzie Pass, we encountered a sign that said "Entering Linn County." Uh-oh. I'd planned to visit Lane County's northeast corner via the Pacific Crest Trail just west of Dee Wright Observatory at McKenzie Pass, thinking that the observatory was right at the Cascade crest and therefore the county line. But I was wrong.

So, once again, we had to take a vote to allow me to briefly leave Lane County, simply out of convenience. After the unanimous vote, we proceeded into Linn County and drove about one-quarter mile more before reaching the southbound PCT trailhead. We still had another quarter of a mile of trail through the lava of Linn County before getting back into Lane County, where we would finally be within a couple of hundred yards of the corner where Linn, Lane, and Deschutes counties all meet. Just as Lane County's southeast corner ends in a toe-like projection into Klamath

County, so Linn County's southeast corner is toe-like and has Deschutes County both north and east of it.

About where the trail crossed from Linn County back into Lane County, we had a splendid view of the rustic Dee Wright Observatory just to our north. The structure, built of lava rock by a group of Civilian Conservation Corps workers in the 1930s, blends so perfectly into its setting that we didn't even notice it at first. And Highway 242 that passes along its south base wasn't visible at all from our vantage point.

Although nature has had several millennia to colonize this lava flow, the vegetation is still extremely sparse. There are plenty of lichens and mosses, but few woody plants and even fewer herbaceous (soft-tissued) plants. Nonetheless, scattered trees grow among the lava, wherever they've found enough soil to eke out a living. There are a few lodgepole pines, mountain hemlocks, and subalpine firs. I am surprised to see, too, a relatively large ponderosa pine perhaps forty feet tall. Ponderosa pine in Oregon has two subspecies: the form found east of the Cascades, and a variant called *Pinus ponderosa* var. *willamettensis*, or valley pine, that grows west of the crest, especially in the southern Willamette Valley. This tree is growing 100 yards or so west of the crest, so is it a valley pine? I somehow doubt it. The nearest seed source for ponderosa pine is only a few miles *east* of here, so this tree is likely the east-side subspecies even though it's growing on the west side of the crest.

It's mid-afternoon and the sky is deep blue. Even with the strong sunshine, though, the air is still bracing, as there's a strong west wind today and the temperature here at some 5,300 feet elevation is a chilly 62 degrees Fahrenheit even without the wind. But it's easy to find windfree and warm spots among the lava, and that's where I've chosen to sit down and write.

In addition to the trees mentioned, there are several other woody plants found here and there in the area. (Again, rough lava dominates the surface, but on suitable sites, a few plants are able to make it.) In some spots, there is pinemat manzanita—a hardy, evergreen groundcover—and an occasional individual of pinemat's more shrub-like relative, green manzanita. A creeping form of juniper grows here as well.

The only animals we've seen are a chipmunk—which likely survives on the conifer seeds produced here and little else—and a Clark's nutcracker, a large jay-like bird that also depends on conifer seeds for most of its diet.

The view from this spot is magnificent, with Belknap Crater and Mount Jefferson to the north, and to the south, North and Middle Sisters which together are hiding from view the South Sister peak. Collier Glacier, the largest glacier this far south in the contiguous states, is nestled between the North and Middle Sisters peaks.

It's time to turn back because the PCT, after entering this corner of Lane County only a couple of hundred yards ago, now leaves it again and enters Deschutes County, where it will remain until it re-enters Lane County near Yapoah Crater, about two-and-a-half miles south of here.

What a simply glorious day to be up here. There's not a car, a building, a power line, or another person—besides those in my group—visible for miles and miles. And no mosquitoes!

ONE THOUSAND DAYS

I'm seated at the base of a young western redcedar tree in a stand of trees I call The Cathedral, where some of the Douglas-fir trees are more than 400 years old. The forest undercanopy is very open except for widely scattered clusters of vine maples, and the forest floor itself is carpeted in most places with Pacific sword-ferns. It's likely an unseasonably warm September day down in the McKenzie Valley, which I left several hours ago, but where I sit here in the shade beneath trees some 200 feet tall, the temperature is barely 70 degrees. A stiff east wind is blowing above the forest canopy, but here on the forest floor, it's nearly calm.

I've come here to celebrate a very important anniversary. Today is the *one thousandth day* that I'm spending "upriver" here in the West Cascades near McKenzie Bridge. Because I'm not the same person I was 31 years ago, when I first visited this area, it's interesting to consider how I've changed through the years—or, rather, how my perceptions and enjoyment of the area's forests and rivers here have changed.

Like my life, my one thousand days here seem to be divisible into four distinct periods: youth, the peripatetic years, settling down, and contentment or reflection time. During my "youthful" years here, the 1980s, I seldom visited the area except by bicycle—and even then, relatively infrequently—as it provided a larger radius for my one-day explorations. With the aid of my bicycle and over time, I went as far east as Sisters (on the other side of the Cascades), as far north as Deer Creek, and as far south as Horsepasture Mountain. But at the same time, I was still exploring other parts of the state and didn't yet consider this area particularly remarkable.

When I switched to exploring this area almost exclusively, and mostly by foot, in the 1990s, I continued to range relatively widely, hiking as far as seven or eight miles some days, and going from canyon-bottom to ridge-top on a regular basis. Although I had a few favorite spots, I wasn't yet in the mood to settle down, and my home territory still covered nearly two square miles.

One year, I kept track of my weekly wanderings on a single map, and at the end of the year, most of the map was simply covered with squiggly lines indicating the multiple routes I'd taken. To be sure, there were some areas that I visited more often than others—The Cathedral being one of them.

As I grew older, I began to settle down and to reduce the radius of my exploration even more. I still wandered a lot; I just didn't wander as far as I had in earlier years. But I was active for most of each day I was up here, except for mealtimes, and times spent in my hammock during the warm months, or basking in the sunshine on sunny winter days.

Finally, however, I reached the stage I referred to earlier as contentment. Most of my visits these days include very little hiking, just enough to get away from highway noise. And the bulk of the day is spent in just one or two places, where I alternately eat, nap, daydream, and write. I can sit for hours at a time in places like The Cathedral here, and not feel the slightest urge to leave, or even to stand up. One day, in fact, I did sit in the same place for nearly eight hours, and described in an essay called "One Square Foot" what I saw happen in that one square foot over the course of the day.

Few people these days have the opportunity for what I call "reflection time," which is precisely what these days alone in the woods provide for me. Three of the characteristics of reflection time are solitude, the lack of distractions, and being outdoors. To meet all three of those criteria, one needs to leave home and go to a place where one is unlikely to encounter anyone else for at least a few hours—if not a day or a week.

Fortunately, here in Oregon, there is an abundance of publicly owned lands—administered primarily by the U.S. Forest Service and the Bureau of Land Management—which can provide the solitude required. During the course of 31 years and 1,000 days in the woods—the vast majority of which have been spent alone and off-road and off-trail—I have encountered only two other people, and those two young men were seen by me on the same afternoon. Approximately half of Oregon's 100,000 square miles are publicly owned, so there are plenty of places to disappear to.

One of the results of having visited one area so many times is that, in addition to getting to know its nooks and crannies, I've "bonded" with it as well and find that being here nurtures my soul like nowhere else can. It's no different than living with someone you truly love for several decades. As time goes by, your love grows ever deeper, and although you might enjoy the company of others from time to time—socially, sexually, or however—those relationships pale in comparison to the one you have with the one you love.

So it is that, over the years, I've become very protective of the bond I have with this West Cascades landscape I call my *Lebensraum* or "living room." It's public land that anyone can visit, of course, and I sometimes bring friends or my young students here to spend the day. However, I ask that they not return to this same area, but instead find their own "special place" among the thousands of square miles of public land with which we Oregonians are blessed. And if they do come back to this area, I ask only that they not tell me beforehand of their plans, nor afterward of their experiences here. I simply don't want to know about it.

One winter, more than a decade ago, a very good Eugene friend reported to me that he'd visited this area and had seen my boot tracks in the snow— from my visit a day or two before his own visit. I was astonished at my reaction to his revelation: I felt as if I'd been violated. And I told my friend that. I couldn't at the time explain the feeling, but eventually I realized that, because of the intimate bond I have with this place, I do not wish to share it with anyone else, unless that person is expressly asked to accompany me for a day or two.

Because of the superior quality of the environment here—fresh air, no distractions, and natural silence (i.e., no, or few, human-made sounds)—I now do almost all of my writing and editing here. I write and edit with a pencil, and then write the second draft on the computer once I return to town. I can still write and edit in town, but it's much more difficult to do effectively there than it is here in the woods.

One thousand days. That's two and three-quarters years of my life so far. I only hope that I can continue my visits to these lovely woods for as many years as I have left on this pleasant planet.

THE NOISIEST BORDER CROSSING

I have to laugh. All I wanted to do is find a somewhat private place away from the roadside here where I might relieve myself. But both sides of the road are wooded, and those woods are protected by impenetrable walls of Himalayan blackberries. And wherever I found a slight break in the blackberries, there was poison-oak—which for me is even more fearsome than the blackberries. At last, I discovered an open spot maybe 150 yards north of the county line where I could safely get into the little woods and find the peace that I sought.

I have to laugh again because, of all the places I've visited in Lane County over these past months, this one is without a doubt the most unpleasant— at least in some ways. Here in this little saddle between fir-covered hills, there are six lanes of asphalt and two steel rails.

To my east is Interstate 5, where northbound trucks labor noisily up the grade and southbound trucks apply their extremely loud compression brakes as they go *down* the hill. And where I'm sitting on the west shoulder of Longview Lane—a two-lane county road that parallels the freeway— huge, smoke-belching trucks zip by every few minutes, hauling rock to the road construction site at the nearby freeway interchange. Finally, not 100 feet west of me are the Union Pacific railroad tracks. No, it's not a place one comes to in search of peace and quiet. But like anywhere else, it does have its beauty if the visitor is intent on finding it, which I am.

(Just now, a southbound helicopter has added its own unique sound to the site's nearly constant cacophony.)

I caught the seven o'clock Cottage Grove bus in downtown Eugene this morning, and just over a half-hour later arrived with my bike at the Village (Shopping) Center. I'd been through Cottage Grove three or four times in the past, but always fleetingly, so I wanted to get to know the town a bit more. From my map, I determined that River Road would be a nice way to get through town by avoiding the commercial and industrial areas and following the Coast Fork of the Willamette River. Indeed, it turned out to be a pleasant little street even at "rush hour" on a Monday morning. For most of its length, the street is separated from the adjacent Coast Fork by trees and grass and a running trail or sidewalk.

Along the way, I decided to wander through an older residential neighborhood where all the east-west streets are named after trees and in alphabetical order, beginning in the south with Ash Street and proceeding through Birch, Chestnut, Dogwood, and Elm to Holly. I chose Birch Street to explore and was pleased with the architectural variety of the houses, some of them dating back to the late 1800s. But my most exciting find was a large pecan tree growing in the park strip on the south side of the street. Pecans are rare in our area, and although the trees grow very well here and cast a lovely shade, their nuts seldom mature because our summer nights are too cool compared to where the trees are native in the south-central U.S.

Back on River Road, I passed a delightful pedestrian-only suspension bridge across the Coast Fork, and the attractive, relatively new Cottage Grove High School. When I reached the junction of River Road with southbound Highway 99, I was within just a few miles of The Border.

As I continued south, beautiful oak-studded, grassy hills where sheep were grazing rose west of the highway. The landscape reminded me of what this area looked like when Euro-Americans first passed through in the mid-1800s. The hills that most places are now covered with Douglas-firs were back then home to a much more open oak savanna. There were certainly conifers here and there, but it wasn't a closed-canopy forest as it is these days. That's because, for thousands of years before the pioneers' arrival, area aborigines set fire to these hills on a regular basis, both to maintain the open landscape—which we humans have favored wherever we've gone on the planet since leaving the savannas of eastern Africa ages ago—as well as to promote the plants and animals on which their economy had come to depend.

It turns out that the beautiful hills I was gazing at are part of the Hawley Ranch that dates back to 1852. In the absence of Indian-set fires, the next best way to maintain an oak savanna in western Oregon is by letting livestock graze it, as they eat the seedlings of any trees that attempt to colonize the open grasslands.

A few minutes after passing the ranch and crossing the railroad tracks, I saw a little sign ahead—Leaving Lane County—which indicated I'd soon be at The Border. As I parked my bike and leaned it up against the sign's four-by-four-inch wooden post, I smiled. The sign was not the only evidence that this was a county border. The asphalt on Longview Lane here has a distinct line across it, indicating where the territory of Lane County's road crew ends, and that of Douglas County begins. It's nice to see that the road crews so rigorously respect this little political boundary.

Interestingly, there is other evidence of the county line along the road's shoulders which, on the Douglas County side of the border, are lined with the leafless branches of blackberries and other plants that dared to grow too close to the road and have been killed by herbicide. But on the Lane County side—where for some years now we've used mowers rather than herbicides to maintain roadside vegetation—the roadside plants are just cut back, but not killed.

I also noticed that behind the tiny sign that faces southbound traffic here and says "Leaving Lane County" is a much larger sign facing *north*bound traffic. To read it, of course, my head would have to leave Lane County. But I decided to peek around anyway, even at the risk of setting off an alarm. The sign says, "Welcome to Lane County—Enjoy Our County Roads." I wonder why Douglas County isn't likewise boasting about *its* roads at this crossing.

Now that it's mid-morning and I've finished my roadside breakfast—rolled oats (with yogurt, milk, apples, raisins, walnuts, honey, and cinnamon), orange juice, and a piece of milk chocolate—I can focus more on characterizing this site. As mentioned above, I'm sitting in the middle of an important transportation corridor that's apparently existed here for millennia. For most of that time, it was an Indian trail. Then, more recently, it was a wagon road, as the Applegate Trail—a southern route to the Willamette Valley that branched off the California Trail in Nevada—passed through here, beginning in 1846. Later, the wagon road became a Territorial Road, when Oregon was still a territory and not yet a state. Later still, the Pacific Highway that stretched from Canada to Mexico was constructed through this same little gap in the hills. Sometime in the 1870s, the railroad was built, connecting the southern Willamette Valley with

California. And in 1966, Interstate 5 was completed, replacing in many sections the Pacific Highway.

Besides all of these vehicles and all of this noise, what else does one find here? Since it's late September and there hasn't been any significant rainfall since June, the landscape is somewhat parched in appearance. But beneath the trees where I found some privacy earlier, I saw the withered and dried stalks of a half-dozen tiger lily plants which back in May evidently graced the forest floor there with their bright orange, recurved petals speckled with black.

At the moment, however, the only plant in bloom is the pretty, sky-blue chicory, a patch of which I'm sitting next to on the roadside here. Like most of the other plants along the road—as well as me—the chicory plants are descendants of immigrants from Europe. They're joined here on this sunny roadside by Queen Anne's lace (the wild progenitor of our cultivated carrots), summer dandelions (*Hypochaeris radicata*), St. John's wort, and several species of Eurasian grasses. There's not a single blade of native grass here, though native bunchgrasses once carpeted the nearby hills, and not so long ago.

A much more recent arrival here is spotted knapweed (*Centaurea maculosa*) which only in the past decade has become an abundant "weed" in our area. It's just another reminder of how extensively we've disturbed native ecosystems by introducing—purposely or, more often, inadvertently— plants from elsewhere, which end up displacing native plants and in many instances (e.g., blackberries) dominating the landscape to the exclusion of other plants.

A little to the north along this shoulder of the road is a patch of yerba buena (*Satureja douglasii*), a native mint with aromatic and evergreen leaves that creeps along the ground. And in the wettest part of the ditch at my side grows the native horsetail. The only other native plant I see here on the road's shoulder is a species of lupine which, even after two months of summer drought, still has rich, green leaves.

The adjacent woodlands consist of red alder, cottonwood, and willow in the lower, seasonally wet areas, and then bigleaf maple, Douglas-fir, and incense-cedar as one moves upslope onto better-drained soil. The trees are all less than fifty years old, having likely seeded in on their own after the completion of the interstate through here, which clearly involved a lot of earth-moving.

There are also a number of Oregon white oaks scattered throughout the area, which confirm for me that oaks dominated these hills until very recently. Because of their large nuts, oaks don't travel across a landscape very far very fast. So if young oaks are currently growing in an area, that indicates that their parents grew close by, too. And the only way their parents could have grown here is if the area had been regularly burned, thus preventing the encroachment of conifers.

As I reached the end of my two hours here at The Border, I was delighted to notice a brief pause in the traffic noise. For just ten or fifteen seconds, there was no traffic at all, either on the adjacent freeway or here along Longview Lane. And I smiled one more time before packing up and heading back to Cottage Grove to meet friends with whom I'll spend the afternoon exploring the Row River Trail before catching the bus back to Eugene in the early evening.

PRESCIENT PARENTS

In an effort to engage the students in my Trees Across Oregon course at the University of Oregon, I often pass tree-related items around the classroom so the students can see, touch, and even smell the items. One day, it might be the hefty seed cone of a Coulter pine. Another day, it could be a stick that a beaver has de-barked to eat the nutritious cambium layer just beneath the bark. Or 50-million-year-old fossilized dawn-redwood leaves from central Oregon. It means so much more to the students to see these things up close than it would if I just projected images on the screen, or drew sketches on the blackboard.

Most of the objects I pass around have a special meaning to me. I acquired the pinecone during a field class I taught in the San Gabriel Mountains of southern California in the late 1980s. The beaver stick I came across while exploring along the Willamette River right in Eugene. The dawn-redwood fossil was given to me by a neighbor boy who, with his family, had visited the town of Fossil, Oregon—yes, there really is such a place—where they dug for fossils in a hillside adjacent to the local high school and happened to come across several fine specimens.

But perhaps the most valuable and meaning-filled possession of mine that I pass around is a little book called *The Golden Nature Guide to Trees*. It was given to me by my parents for my eighth birthday. I'm sure I looked at it now and again through my youth, and into my Boy Scout years, but then I forgot about it. Many years later, I came across the book when going through things at my parents' house, and I brought it back with me to Oregon.

Just inside the cover is inscribed, in my mother's handwriting: *To Dennis Lueck—8 yrs old—July 9, 1960, from Daddy and Mother.* Little could they have known that, one day, I'd be teaching a course about trees at the university. Or was there in fact something about me that led them to believe I'd find the book useful, and maybe want to know more someday about the trees that grew all around us? But they never gave tree books to any of my siblings. Why not? What was it about me that was different?

At that time, we lived in the small town of Jersey Shore in the mountains of north-central Pennsylvania. (The word Pennsylvania actually means Penn's Woods—after the family of the state's Quaker founder, William Penn—because it was once almost 100 percent forested.) I recall a childhood where we were free to roam, unlike many of today's children, and I roamed far and wide, at least within the hilltop neighborhood where we lived. Between our house and the high school at the bottom of the hill was a woods, where I spent much time. I also was constantly on the lookout for nesting birds, and during the breeding season from mid-spring to mid-summer, knew where most of the bird nests were within a couple-hundred-yard radius of our house. I explored mostly on my own and of course climbed trees, when necessary, to peer into nests I'd spotted from the ground.

My siblings also spent time outside, but I don't think that my parents considered any of them especially interested in nature. I was evidently the sole "nature boy" and how I ended up like this, I suppose I'll never really know. But my love for the outdoors, whatever its source, was clearly nurtured by my parents, and the tree book—as well as many other gifts through the years—is evidence of that.

More than fifty years later, in the community where I chose to make my home, many people refer to me as "the tree guy"—even though I maintain that I am a "whole" person and not just a tree guy. During my early years of underemployment in Eugene, I spent countless hours bicycling the streets and alleys and looking at the trees. I was especially interested in the less commonly planted trees and rejoiced whenever I stumbled upon one. And I have always been fascinated to think about how trees came to grow where they do. Every tree, like every person, has a story to tell. Unfortunately, trees can't talk—or perhaps we just don't yet know how to understand what they've been trying to tell us for so long.

Over the years, though, I've discovered the stories of many of our local trees by talking with my elders and by poring over old photographs, and I enjoy telling others what I've found. From 1987–1998, I researched and led monthly "tree walks" between April and November, where attendees and I would explore a Eugene neighborhood's trees—a different neighborhood each month. It became quite a social event for many people and something they looked forward to. Attendance probably averaged about 50 people, but I recall one tour in the South University Neighborhood where there were 116 tree lovers along. That was a bit unwieldy, but people seemed to have a good time nonetheless.

I've planted and overseen the planting of hundreds of trees around Eugene over the years, and I've often found myself publicly advocating for their preservation when "development" threatened. A few times I was successful; most times I was not. But each time I said something in defense of trees, I planted another seed in someone's mind about the benefits and wonders of trees, and that ripple effect is far more important in the long run than the preservation of an individual tree.

In 1997, I cofounded Eugene Tree Foundation—now Friends of Trees Eugene—and for more than a decade I wrote most of the lead articles for the organization's quarterly newsletter and served as its editor. And I have worked with City of Eugene urban forestry staff to improve the quality of care that trees around the community receive.

Besides teaching "the trees class" at the university, I continue to advocate for trees. Most recently, I took a stand in defiance of University planners who elected to remove one of the largest and oldest London plane-trees in Oregon, just so the campus student union could be enlarged. I give a half-dozen campus tree tours every year to both public and private groups, and I continue to plant and care for trees both on my own property and in my neighborhood.

Regardless of how my parents knew so long ago that this was the path down which I'd one day walk, it's a path I've enjoyed walking along for several decades now. And since my parents are no longer living, it doesn't look like I'll ever again receive another little book—on a different subject—that might risk diverting my attention from this path I so dearly love.

WHITE-FRONTED GEESE

It's the last week of September and I'm spending three days and two nights alone here in the West Cascades before classes begin at the university next Monday and my life becomes a little more hectic for a while. I'm camped in a stand of old trees, far from the noise of any streams or rivers or highways, so it's extremely quiet and I can hear sounds that might go unnoticed in other places or under different circumstances.

Last night, my first night here, I blew out my candle lantern here in my tent around 11 p.m., and fell asleep to the sound of raindrops hitting the fly of the tent. It had rained fairly steadily for much of the day—our first real rain after our annual summer drought here in Western Oregon—but the rain tapered off about mid-evening. In fact, it might have been just drips from the forest canopy I was hearing rather than actual raindrops.

I slept soundly for at least several hours, and when I awoke once during the night, I heard geese flying over: white-fronted geese, whose call I recognize. I'm accustomed to seeing them fly over the West Cascades the last week of April most every year—sometimes in enormous flocks of hundreds of birds—and I've also seen them over my house in Eugene during the day, or heard them fly over at night.

In spring, they fly in a northwesterly direction past here, so I presume they're coming from Klamath Lake, or possibly Summer Lake, both of which are in south-central Oregon. They turn north once they reach the Willamette Valley, and eventually arrive at their breeding grounds on the tundra of Alaska and northernmost Canada. At this season, they're doing the exact opposite, so they are headed southeast across the Cascades.

Their migration is quite dramatic, as it's very intense for a short period, and then it's over. I hadn't heard or seen any white-fronted geese this fall until last night. But as I lay here in my tent, I heard flock after flock pass over, each one separated from the other by a period of only a few minutes. When I finally awoke after dawn, they were still flying over, although the flocks were spaced farther apart.

I packed up to go farther up the ridge to have my breakfast, and there, too, I heard flock after flock. I seldom saw the birds, even when I was out in the open, because they fly extremely high, and the light conditions today made it difficult to see even the commercial jets that fly over here, say nothing of a flock of relatively tiny geese.

There seemed to be a pause in their passage midday, as I heard none for several hours. Then mid-afternoon, things picked up again and now, mid-evening, the flocks continue to pass. To give the reader an idea of the frequency with which the geese pass, I noted the times I heard them just before making my dinner—when the noise of my stove prevents me from hearing them—and just after. And this is what I found: flights at 18:47 (6:47 p.m.), 18:49, 18:52, 18:58 (then dinnertime), 20:08, 20:38, 20:48, 20:52, 21:00, 21:12, and 21:21.

The flocks I was able to see today consisted of between 100 and 200 individuals. Let's say the average number of birds per flock is 150, and I've heard well over a hundred flocks since last night. That's at least 15,000 birds right there! They all seem to fly almost directly overhead here. But is their migration corridor across the Cascades a wide one, so I'm seeing only a small portion of the population? I don't think so, as I'd be able when out in the open to notice flocks flying just a little north or a bit south of here, and I haven't seen any. It's incredible to believe that the migration corridor of this species of goose is so narrow—following closely the McKenzie River Valley and then passing near the Three Sisters peaks before turning south to Klamath Lake—but why not?

The marvel of animal migration has long fascinated me—from marine mammals such as the Pacific gray whale, to monarch butterflies and chinook salmon. Thankfully, I get to see (or at least hear) the white-fronted geese almost every year, usually in spring. As far as I can recall, this is the first time I've witnessed their fall migration from right here. At any rate, when there is so much news about how our planet and its natural systems are under siege, it's reassuring for me to know that the white-fronted geese, at least, are keeping to the same schedule and route they've apparently had for a long, long time.

SOUNDS OF THE FOURTH DAY OF FALL
Aural Snapshot No. 25

One of these days, I'm going to do an aural snapshot in an urban area—likely Eugene—but for now, I'm keeping to the "wilds" of the West Cascades, where human-caused sounds are relatively few and the sounds of the rest of the natural world tend to dominate.

As usual, I sat down with my clipboard and my watch-with-a-second-hand and noted, for each minute of one hour, the different sounds I heard during that minute, whether the sound occurred only once, was repetitive, or was continuous.

This snapshot took place on Wednesday, 24 September—between 11:56 a.m. and 12:55 p.m.—at an elevation of about 2,000 feet in the middle of a broad ridge in the West Cascades, a couple of miles east of McKenzie Bridge. It was partly sunny, with an air temperature of 56 degrees Fahrenheit.

I heard an amazing variety of sounds this time, most of them birds, as usual. Here's the tally, in descending order from the sounds I heard most often during the 60 minutes, to the sounds I heard the least:

35 minutes	machine noise
34 minutes	fly
17 minutes	red-breasted nuthatch
15 minutes	jet
15 minutes	pileated woodpecker
15 minutes	golden-crowned kinglet

13 minutes	chickaree
10 minutes	flicker
10 minutes	robin
7 minutes	chickadee
6 minutes	frog
6 minutes	back-up beeper
4 minutes	junco
3 minutes	varied thrush
2 minutes	woodpecker tapping
2 minutes	mosquito
2 minutes	helicopter
2 minutes	yellowjacket
2 minutes	Steller's jay
2 minutes	red crossbill
1 minute	evening grosbeak
1 minute	truck
1 minute	gray jay
1 minute	sapsucker

That's a total of 206 "sound-minutes"—the number of minutes during which a particular sound was heard at least once—of which 59 were machine-related, 38 were insects, 13 were chickarees, and 6 were frogs (a total of 116). The remaining 90 sound-minutes were from 13 different species of birds, all of which I was able to identify by only their calls or songs.

The variety of birds I heard was perhaps due to my sitting at an *ecotone*—with a stand of dense, old, fir forest behind me, and in front of me a recently thinned stand of fifty-year-old firs. In other words, I was at the edge of two distinctly different habitats. Pileated woodpeckers, golden-crowned kinglets, and chickarees—small squirrels native to this area—prefer the older stand, while juncos, sapsuckers, robins, and flies prefer the sunnier, more open areas.

The distant sounds of machinery were, it turns out, from a road crew working more than a mile away from me along Horse Creek Road—which lies in a canyon about 500 feet in elevation below this ridge. But sound travels up and out from its source, and with few other sounds to compete in such a naturally quiet setting as this, the noise from vehicles and machinery was very audible, even at such a distance.

LANE COUNTY'S *OTHER* THREE SISTERS

Since Lane County's creation in 1851, Eugene—originally Eugene City—has been the county seat and the site of the county courthouse. A nicely restored version of the first "courthouse," built in 1853, can be seen just outside the Lane County Historical Museum at the fairgrounds in Eugene. That little wooden building's successors, however, were not so fortunate. Each was erected, then later destroyed to make way for the newer-and-bigger courthouse, until the current iteration at the southeast corner of East Seventh Avenue and Oak Street was built in 1959—the same year its predecessor (built in 1898) at the northeast corner of Eighth and Oak was torn down.

In 1976, a new Public Service Building was dedicated next to the courthouse. This building, designed by the local firm of Unthank Seder Poticha Architects, is one of my favorite public buildings in Lane County, with its combination of wood, concrete, glass, local basalt rock, and sheet metal. I'm especially fond of the huge, airy, sky-lit atrium that extends in an L-shape through the building's interior.

But my favorite part of the entire building—which takes up more than half of a city block—is the above-grade courtyard near the building's southwest entrance. Every spring, when I bring my Trees Across Oregon class—which I teach for the University of Oregon's Department of Landscape Architecture—for a tour of downtown Eugene, we begin our visit at the Public Service Building so I can show them the magnificent trio of trees growing right out of the middle of the building.

We walk in the main entrance and up a short flight of stairs to a large landing at the southwest corner of the central atrium, where I stand at the railing and the class faces the atrium. I make a few comments about the building's overall design, its history, and the choice of materials used in the construction. Then I tell them to turn around and look outside. And they think, "Outside? But we're in the middle of the building!" As they turn around, then, they see through the floor-to-ceiling windows into the courtyard from which the Three Sequoia Sisters send their magnificent trunks and canopies skyward. There are always little gasps of surprise and awe, and some students wonder afterward how they didn't even notice the huge trees as they climbed the short flight of stairs—along a tall window looking into the courtyard—to our first stop in the atrium.

I ask the class, of course, what kind of trees they are, and how old they think they might be. Many assume that the building was built *around* three already-existing trees. But, I point out, that couldn't be, as the courtyard is a good five feet above the site's natural valley-floor grade. Instead, the trees were planted just after the building's completion.

But giant sequoias (*Sequoiadendron giganteum*) grow very, very well here in the Upper Willamette Valley, as our climate closely resembles that of the mid-elevation Sierra Nevada of California where they are native. The summers there, as here, are dry and very warm, but infrequently hot. And the winters in both places are wet and relatively mild, with daytime highs above freezing most days.

Most importantly, these three trees were provided with an ample volume of soil for them to be able to develop to their full potential. The courtyard itself is about 30 feet by 40 feet, and the trees' roots have certainly filled that entire area by now, and at least some of the roots likely reach down several feet or more, perhaps even to the native soil at the base of the building, provided the soil they're growing in is sufficiently well-drained.

Some years, in anticipation of our visit, I ask a building custodian to unlock the courtyard's access door so that after viewing the Three Sequoia Sisters from above and from inside the building, we can see them at courtyard level and out in the fresh air. There is no public access to the courtyard itself. About the only time people use it, I understand, is when civil ceremony weddings take place in the building and the wedding party wishes to have its photo taken somewhere outside.

Today, however, I got permission to spend some time alone in the courtyard, just to get a better sense of this place that I call the "navel" of Lane County. That is, Eugene is near the geographical center of Lane County; the Public Service Building is near the center of Eugene; and the courtyard is near the center of the Public Service Building. It just makes sense, doesn't it?

From noon until about 1 p.m., I've been sitting on a chair here on the little brick terrace in the southwest corner of the courtyard—occasionally getting up to walk around a bit—and just observing my surroundings in this place that's so special to me. It's a sunny and warm October afternoon, and even though I'm near city center and busy Seventh Avenue, it's relatively quiet here. That's one of the wonderful characteristics of courtyards in general. And if there were a little fountain or some other moving water here, it would be even more pleasant, as that soothing sound would distract visitors from other, more intrusive, sounds. But there's no fountain here.

I have been serenaded the entire hour by several European starlings evidently enjoying the sunny afternoon from the tops of the sequoias. Starlings are both great singers as well as mimics of other birds, but today their repertoire has consisted mostly of singing, with very few imitations. At one point, a scrub jay holding an acorn in its beak flew into the courtyard. The bird proceeded to bury the acorn in the duff of dead and fallen needles beneath the sequoias. In fact, there are half a dozen young English oaks growing in the courtyard, from acorns placed here in other years and forgotten by the jays that planted them. The source of these acorns is almost certainly the streetside columnar English oaks both east and south of Eugene's city hall, which takes up the city block just to the east of this one.

A little bit ago, a crow landed atop the nearby courthouse and announced its presence with a few caws. I could see it from here, but it apparently had no interest—at least not today—in visiting this isolated courtyard.

The plants other than the seedling oaks here in the courtyard are a real mixture. There's a struggling groundcover of periwinkle (*Vinca minor*), as well as a solitary English laurel and a lone Japanese fatsia—both of them clearly unhappy with their circumstances. And adjacent to a little head-high sculpture that seems to me completely out of place here, are six dwarf boxwood bushes that also seem very much out of place, in two straight rows, each with three evenly-spaced boxwood plants.

As a horticulturist and naturalist, I can't help but think how truly beautiful this courtyard could be, and what an asset to the building, if it just received a little regular attention from someone who understood plants and their needs and had a good sense of design. The sequoias are holding their own, but they're beginning to look a little potbound now at age forty or so, and could benefit from a few more nutrients (i.e., fertilizer). And a large tub or two of seasonally interesting flowers atop the brick terrace here would be a nice addition as well.

Dream on, Whitey. As is usually the case these days in our culture, what are essential amenities to some of us are thought to be expensive and expendable luxuries to others. As a county, we spend tens of millions of dollars every year building and maintaining roads, buildings, parking lots, and the like—but a tiny courtyard like this, the navel of our county, goes wanting for a few hundred dollars' worth of upgrading and upkeep. It's a sad comment on what we as a community consider important.

Not 100 feet from here, another fantastic space—much bigger than this courtyard—is going to waste. It's the huge rooftop "plaza" atop the east side of this building. It could be an attractive and inviting rooftop garden or green roof. Instead, it's a bleak, uninviting space dominated by concrete and the noise of passing traffic. What a pity.

Inside the building, the lovely, green curtains of *pothos*—a trailing houseplant—that once cascaded from the railings of the atrium's upper level have disappeared. I'm told it was because the plants became diseased. That's something that happens sometimes to indoor plants, of course, especially if they're an extensive monoculture, as these plants were. But usually, you cure the disease, or remove the infected plants and start over. Instead, the plants have been eliminated, with apparently no thought of replacing them.

In the aforementioned ways—in the courtyard, the outdoor plaza, and the atrium—we see a chipping away at the beauty and the environmental health of our county's principal public building. It doesn't bode well for the future. But as long as such amenities are considered a waste of money—"in these difficult economic times," as we've been wont to say now for at least several decades—we will continue to see a diminishment of our cultivated landscapes here in Lane County.

But back to the courtyard and to happier thoughts! Each of the four sides of the nearly-square courtyard is different. The west one, except for the door, is all stucco-like wall. The north one—with the window by the short flight of stairs mentioned earlier—is a combination of stucco, glass, metal, and concrete, as are the east and south sides, but in different proportions. The lower part of the south window actually looks into (and out of) Harris Hall, but the few times I've been in Harris Hall for public meetings, it's been after dark, so I had no idea one could view the Three Sequoia Sisters from inside.

The east wall here has an especially interesting bank of sloped glass windows, so if one looks up from the building's interior that is at street level, one sees into the canopies of the sequoias. It's beautiful! How delightful that the courtyard and these three trees are visible from so many different sides and angles. I credit the building's architects with making it possible.

Although I've spent my time here looking *in* to the building's interior from the outside, I'm aware that a few passersby have looked *out* at me from the inside. But the fact is, most people who pass by this courtyard from inside the building don't even notice it. And of course, virtually no one passing *outside* the building, along Oak Street or Eighth Avenue, has any idea the courtyard is even here. That's one of the reasons I like it so much: It's a wonderful surprise waiting to be discovered here at the very center of Lane County.

*   *   *   *   *

(*Nota bene*: For readers who are unfamiliar with Lane County—and for Lane County residents who may be a bit geographically "challenged"— there are three snow-capped volcanoes that line the eastern edge of Lane County and are called the Three Sisters. All three peaks reach over 10,000 feet above sea level, and they are visible from many places in Eugene, including—you'll have to take my word for it—from the tops of the Three *Sequoia* Sisters.)

A LANDSCAPE SHAPED BY FIRE AND ICE

It's difficult to say which of my senses is the most overwhelmed here. The view is splendid beyond words, and extends from western Oregon's Coast Range in the west to central Oregon's Newberry Crater in the east, and then north to Mount Hood. In the middle-ground—between this peak and the Three Sisters—lies that sapphire of the High Cascades, Waldo Lake. And for miles and miles, up one ridge and down into the next valley, the landscape is carpeted in every direction with countless conifers.

But what I hear is equally remarkable, because I can hear nothing except a slight breeze that picks up occasionally. And a few minutes ago, several mountain chickadees stopped by to say hello.

With the breeze and a temperature of only 58 degrees here at an elevation of over 7,000 feet, I'm pleased to be sitting in the sunshine on this October day. Despite the relatively cool temperature, I feel very comfortable and am wearing only a light jacket—plus the rest of my clothes, of course.

I can't remember if I've ever actually been here before. While I was making plans for this trip and studying maps, I seemed to recall coming here with the Obsidians hiking club sometime in the mid-1980s. But I have no photographs of that outing, and I always carried a camera with me back then. If it were a cloudy or wet day, however, I might not have taken any photos, as the view I have today might not have been visible then. No matter.

Nearly twenty miles away and a little west of north, several small smoke plumes rise vertically from a forested ridge. There are currently no forest fires burning in that area, so I'm guessing that the U. S. Forest Service is doing some prescribed burning. It looks like the Chucksney Mountain area, where I know there were plans to re-introduce fire—controlled burns, in this case—into that ecosystem from which fire has been absent too long, due to our fire suppression policies of the past century.

Far to the east, beyond the gentle north flank of Newberry Crater, another much larger plume of smoke rises. This must be a range fire in Oregon's high desert country east of Bend. It's clearly too big to be a prescribed burn.

Where I've settled down here on the northwest edge of this mountain's broad summit, I can see many peaks that are familiar to me. Starting in the south and moving north, they are: Maiden Peak, Mount Ray, The Twins, Charlton Butte, Bachelor Butte, Broken Top, South Sister, Middle Sister—with Middle Sister hiding North Sister from this perspective—Mount Washington, Three Fingered Jack, Mount Jefferson, and Mount Hood. That's quite a line-up.

The peak I'm by far the most familiar with is Bachelor, where I lived for two summers in 1978 and 1979, and visited regularly during the other seasons. I had a field camp at the 8,000-foot level on the butte's north slope where I was studying the ecology of whitebark pine for my Masters thesis at Oregon State University.

Besides fires that are currently burning—one of them evidently a controlled burn and the other probably a wildfire—there is plenty of evidence of *past* fires here, as well, since fire shapes these conifer forests more than any other disturbance. Along the north shore of Waldo Lake is an extensive silver-white patch—the dead, now bark-less tree trunks remaining from the August 1996 Charlton Butte fire.

Some signs of past fires in this area are more subtle. On the north slope of Maiden Peak, for example, an almost straight line is visible, to the right of which the forest is a darker green with many deep shadows. But left of the line the forest is a much lighter hue of green and very few shadows are visible, because this is a stand of younger and shorter trees. The line indicates, then, the limit of the most recent wildfire which may have occurred as much as a century or more ago.

(The silence that I've been enjoying has now been sullied by the arrival of both a commercial jet and a cargo plane. These aircraft will quickly pass, but the interruption does not go unnoticed.)

Besides fire, this landscape has been shaped by ice. On our way here this morning, we stopped maybe a quarter of a mile short of the trailhead to have our breakfasts. I chose a grass-covered outcropping with a lovely view to the south, where I sat down to enjoy both the quiet of the High Country in fall as well as my meal. The bedrock exposed at my side was quite smooth, but it was also incised with numerous parallel grooves that all pointed downhill. A glacier clearly moved down the southwest flank of this peak during the most recent Ice Age, which reached its maximum extent in this area about 14,000 years ago. The striations were created by rocks embedded at the base of the ice. Beneath the enormous weight of the glacier, the rocks carried in the glacier etched the bedrock across which the ice was moving.

From this peak, one can also gaze into Black Creek canyon, just a few miles northwest of here, with its classic U-shaped cross-section, evidence of past glaciation. An unglaciated stream valley usually has a V-shaped cross-section; only after a glacier passes down it does it acquire its more rounded bottom and steepened sides. Indeed, there is plenty of evidence that the ice sheet that covered the High Cascades plateau from about Mount Jefferson to Mount Mazama (now Crater Lake) was 2,000 or more feet thick at glacial maximum, and included many "tongues" of glacial ice that descended into adjacent valleys both west and east of the Cascades. Some of those tongues excavated depressions that, once the ice "retreated," simply filled with water. Long, narrow Suttle Lake near Santiam Pass, and Odell Lake, of the same shape, just southeast of this peak near Willamette Pass, are two examples.

The area north of Waldo Lake is studded with ponds and lakes of every size which are also glacier-created depressions that filled with water after the ice melted. But Waldo Lake itself—the second deepest in the state—is thought to be a rift-valley lake created by faulting, not glaciation, and the lake already existed long before glaciation ever began. Most of the best-known rift-valley lakes in the world are in eastern Africa, including the huge Lake Tanganyika.

One of the best parts of coming here was hiking through the beautiful forest of 300- to 400-year-old mountain hemlocks about midway between the trailhead and the summit. The forest understory is nearly devoid of vegetation, so one can see a long way into the forest—and also hike off-trail very easily, should one wish to. Interestingly, the summit, at over 7,000 feet elevation, completely lacks whitebark pines, a species I know very well and somewhat expected to see here, as it grows abundantly on The Twins on the far side of Waldo Lake, which are at about the same elevation. But such is the nature of plant—and animal—distribution: not every suitable habitat has necessarily been "discovered" by the species that *could* thrive there. Maybe the next century will see the arrival of the pines, the seeds of which are distributed almost exclusively by a jay-like bird of high elevations called the Clark's nutcracker.

Just before leaving this pleasant perch where I've spent the past two hours, I mentioned tongue-in-cheek to my friend Keiko—who accompanied me here and who grew up in Japan—that I was under the impression that there was a mountain in Japan that had taken its name from this Cascade peak we call Fuji Mountain. But Keiko claims that it was Japan's Fuji which was named first, and this peak took its name from the Japanese one! Well, she's both right and wrong. She's right that the name of Japan's stunningly symmetrical volcano was in fact named long before this peak. But she is wrong about Lane County's Fuji Mountain being named after Japan's Fuji. Although the name is said to date back to sometime before World War II, its origin remains unclear. But one thing is certain: it was *not* named for Japan's Fuji, which it does not resemble at all.

Still, I'm happy to now be able to tell friends that, during the year of my confinement here in Lane County, I was able to climb not one, but two "foreign peaks": Mount Popocatépetl in the Coast Range (see the essay, "My Ascent of El Popo") and Fuji Mountain here in the Cascades.

SITTING ON A DEFUNCT RAILROAD

I need to come back here at dawn, before the noise starts. It's late afternoon now, and this otherwise splendid setting in the middle of a grass-seed field—where Lane County meets Linn County just north of Coburg—is marred only by the sound of back-up beepers at an industrial site about a mile southwest of me. Such a business seems to me incompatible with this otherwise bucolic rural area, but who am I to say?

I'm a sometimes city boy from Eugene, the largest city in Lane County, which lies fourteen miles away at the foot of the prominent peak named Spencer Butte (2,065 feet elevation) that I can see from here. Back in the mid-1800s, the peak was often referred to as "Our Pilot" as it was visible from such a distance north of Eugene that it served to guide settlers back home after trips to points north (e.g., to Salem or to Oregon City). At that time, there weren't yet any roads in the valley to guide travelers and because most of the southern Willamette Valley was still treeless prairie, one could depend on distant topographical features for direction.

But even without Spencer Butte as my guide, I know where the points of the compass are here because many of the roads follow section lines and run due east-west or north-south. In fact, the border separating Lane from Linn County—just a few inches behind me—is right on the line between sections 5 and 8 of Township 16 South Range 3 West.

I came here by bus and by bike this mid-October afternoon because a south wind had picked up, and I looked forward to a nice tailwind to carry me from Coburg to here, a distance of about five miles. Indeed, it was a very easy ride. I locked my bike under an Oregon ash tree at the end of a short gravel road that heads north from Herman Road—which itself lies between

118

North Coburg Road and Powerline Road. I wanted to come here so I could sit on the now-abandoned, narrow-gauge railroad right-of-way that carried passengers and freight between Springfield and Brownsville back in the late 1800s. Indeed, from my vantage point, I can look south across about one quarter of a mile of grass-seed field, and see on the other side of Herman Road the still unvacated railroad bed. Between there and here, however, the right-of-way has long ago been vacated, and there's barely any sign that a railroad once existed. But I know better.

Just to the north of me, at the edge of another grass-seed field, the ground is covered with rocks which were evidently the roadbed for the railway. And most interesting of all, I found sitting there at the side of the field an unusually large, rounded boulder about knee high, and maybe a foot across. Such large boulders do not naturally occur here on this ancient Willamette River floodplain, but rather much smaller "cobbles," mostly of grayish basalt, brought down over the eons from the West Cascades.

But this boulder is blond in color, with shiny sparkles in it. I'm not sure what kind of rock it is, but it is definitely not from the nearby Cascade Mountains. I suspect, in fact, that it's a so-called *glacial erratic* that was entombed in glacial ice 12–15,000 years ago or so, and freighted to this spot in an iceberg that was carried down the Columbia River during the massive Missoula Floods that resulted when an ice dam in western Montana broke and released an enormous volume of iceberg-filled water that then tore across southeastern Washington and down the Columbia Gorge. When the floodwaters receded that had backed up into the Willamette Valley—almost as far south as Eugene—due to a bottleneck in the Columbia downriver from Portland, they left behind many icebergs that, as they melted, released the rocks that had been incorporated into the ice back in present-day Idaho or Montana.

On one hand, that sounds too fantastic to be true. Yet twenty years ago, I found a much smaller piece of granite in a field near Cheshire, so my conclusion about this boulder may not be so preposterous after all. And many other "exotic" rocks have been found throughout the Willamette Valley since Euro-American settlement in the mid-1800s.

Thanks to the substantial rain that fell on 24 September, the grass seeds in this field germinated immediately and, in the warm days since then, the young plants have already attained a height of several inches, creating a bright green sward that stretches in every direction.

To my east rises the steep west flank of the Coburg Hills, with Mount Tom, one of the highest points in the Coburgs at 3,320 feet, very visible. To the south-southeast is Spores Point which looms above the north side of the McKenzie River, not far from the site of the ferry that Jacob Spores operated across the McKenzie in the 1800s. I already mentioned Spencer Butte to the south. And far to the west is the beautiful Coast Range, over which a mass of leaden clouds is now passing—perhaps there will be rain again by morning.

My favorite topographical features visible from here are three buttes to the southeast, at the base of the Coburg Hills. From north to south, they are Rock Hill, Centennial Butte, and Lenon Hill. Of the three, Centennial Butte is by far the most remarkable because of the story associated with its naming. Apparently, the very symmetrical little butte was still treeless in the 1870s, and to celebrate the nation's centennial in 1876, the little girls of the family that lived near the base of the butte planted a circle of maples—and a couple of Douglas-firs, too—at the top of the butte. It's said that they carried buckets of well water up the butte in summer to water their little trees until they became established.

Several decades ago, after hearing this story, I proceeded to visit the butte on my own and marvel at the trees which were then just over a century old. They weren't very big, considering their age, as the soil at the butte's summit is thin and rocky, and incredibly parched in summer. But they were alive, and the circle remains! Since their planting, other trees, mostly firs, have moved onto the butte's north flank on their own, but passing motorists on I-5 can still clearly see the circle of trees at the top.

My reverie about Centennial Butte has suddenly been broken by the whirring sound of a large machine in the Linn County field just northeast of where I sit, which is barely visible behind a wall of Himalayan blackberries. When I stood up and walked over to see what was going on, I saw a large tracked machine with a big tank on it. As it sped eastward across the field, a fan-shaped plume of whitish material spewed from it. Presumably, the field is being fertilized.

In addition to the sound of machinery, both near and far, I'm joined here in the late afternoon by a flock of singing European starlings that have come to feed on the ripe apples in several old trees in a nearby hedgerow. Occasionally, I hear a flicker call, and now and then a towhee. Perhaps the most pleasant sounds, though, are the lacewings that have begun singing just since my arrival. Although sometimes mistaken for crickets—which make a similar but intermittent sound by rubbing their legs together—the lacewing song is continuous and lasts for many seconds, and the insects make the sound by rubbing their silvery, membranous wings together.

Two other birds I've heard but not seen while sitting here are song sparrows and golden-crowned sparrows, both of which are lovely singers. The song of the golden-crowned is particularly sweet, and is typically a series of three descending notes that sound like, "Oh, dear me!" These sparrows breed far to the north of our area, and then winter here in the Upper Willamette Valley—and elsewhere, of course. They're a common wintertime bird both in rural areas, where they frequent the hedgerows separating cultivated fields, as well as in urban and suburban landscapes that provide similar cover and food resources for them.

I'm a little uncomfortable sitting here at the edge of this grass-seed field, as the field's border—like most around here—is a completely dead zone where herbicide has been sprayed to eliminate all other vegetation. This is done to help ensure that the grass seed, when harvested, will have as few impurities in it as possible; that is, it will be free of seeds from other plants that were growing nearby.

Few urban dwellers know much about grass-seed production other than, perhaps, the fact that Lane and Linn counties are both big producers. But what is the grass seed used for and who buys it? Half a dozen different species and cultivated varieties of grass seed are produced in our area, and they end up in lawns, pastures, and golf courses around the world—plus they're used to seed the freshly exposed soil along roadsides and construction sites, to produce a turf mat that will help reduce soil erosion.

In spite of the machinery noise today, this is one of my favorite landscapes in Lane County. Yes, it's the antithesis of the wild landscapes we see most anywhere else in the county. Instead of a diversity of native plants, animals, and insects, it's an ecologically dysfunctional monoculture of a plant (grass) that is originally from Eurasia. But I really savor the expansive view that these huge fields afford.

And I can't wait to return this coming winter when, if I'm lucky, I might find that a flock of blindingly white tundra swans has decided to stop by for a meal of grass. The magnificent birds winter in this area, spending their nights on the water at Fern Ridge Reservoir and their days feeding in grass-seed fields like this one. It is a sight to behold when a flock of the huge white birds descends from a sapphire winter sky and settles gently onto the bright green grass below.

WHY I HATE CARS

I grew up in a culture dominated by cars, where virtually every household owned one or more of them, and where most people's lives were organized around cars. As a youth, I got a driver's permit as soon as I was old enough, and just after my sixteenth birthday, I finally had my own driver's license. I never did drive much, but when I did, it gave me the feeling of absolute freedom to go anywhere I chose—as long as my father agreed to let me use the family car for that usually short period of time. I never thought of driving a car as a privilege, but as a right. It was a part of growing up and, in the absence of any decent public transportation in the small city in Pennsylvania where I lived, driving a car was the most logical and convenient way to get around.

Somewhere along the way, however, I swerved off the road down which I was headed, and ended up leading a very different life than most other people: a largely car-free life. Although I still have a driver's license and I occasionally drive or ride in other people's cars—and drive rented or state-owned vans for my field classes—I've never owned a car and I never will. What happened? Why and how did I choose a path that so few other people in my society have chosen?

First of all, I need to make clear that my carless life is not at all one of deprivation. I go everywhere I want to go, but I just get there without a car. I live what appears to others to be a pretty middle-class existence, but I don't have a car parked in front of my house; I don't even have a driveway or a garage.

I once came really close to buying a car, but I ended up changing my mind. It was 1981, and I'd just gotten my first real job as a horticulturist for the

Portland (Oregon) Parks Bureau. The job came with what I considered to be an unbelievably high salary of $22,000 per year. With that kind of money, I could easily afford a car, so I began reading books about how to buy one. I was almost set on getting a blue Toyota Celica, until I read a book that included a chapter entitled, "Do I Really Need a Car?" It suggested that there are certain circumstances when it is wiser to *rent* a car than to buy one, particularly if one is living in an urban environment with other transportation options (e.g., bus and bicycle) and not using the car to get around during the week. Why have an expensive new car sitting on the street or in a garage, depreciating in value and costing insurance, when you really needed a car only on weekends?

That made sense to me. Throughout my years at college, and the three years I lived in Europe, a bicycle had met most of my needs. And I planned to continue bicycling to work and on errands, once I moved to Portland. So I decided not to buy a car, and to rent one instead, as needed.

During the six months that I lived in Portland, however, it turned out that I never once rented a car. For weekend outings, I depended instead on friends to provide transportation, or I simply took advantage of the hiking opportunities afforded by some of the larger, wilder parks in the Portland area, to which I could bicycle or take a bus.

When it finally came time for me to settle down permanently, I purposely chose a bike-friendly, small city with a mild winter climate, mostly flat terrain, and an excellent transit system. It is also located on a major north-south corridor and has very good intercity bus and train service, and even a good airport. That place, of course, is Eugene, Oregon.

Having demonstrated that I can live a productive and satisfying life myself without a car, I was hopeful that I might persuade others to adopt my carless lifestyle, but I haven't been very successful. Although I have many friends and colleagues who ride bicycles to and from their jobs, and even for some or many in-town errands, everyone I know still owns one or more cars. I've realized that I chose the easy way to go carless, by never owning one in the first place. But because people who already own cars have organized at least a part of their lives around the car and its undisputed convenience, they find that convenience extremely difficult to give up. Or, for their own personal reasons, they see no *need* to give up the car(s). In short, they haven't come to *hate* cars, as I have.

Hate is a very strong word, and I hesitated to use it in the title of this essay, but my feelings toward privately owned automobiles are themselves very strong. Every day I spend in the city, I am subjected to the negative consequences of car ownership. And although I make an effort not to be obsessed by it, it upsets me so much sometimes that, under my breath usually, I say, "I hate cars!" The comfort and convenience that they provide for most everyone else results in a great deal of *dis*comfort and *in*convenience for me, as a non-car owner having to live in the same community with so many of them.

So what exactly is it about privately owned automobiles that I find so annoying or troubling?

The Carnage (pun intended)

Every year in the U.S., nearly 40,000 people are killed in automobile crashes, and several hundred thousand are disabled for life. Every year! Worldwide, fatalities alone are estimated to be 1.25 million people per year.

Add to that the ghastly toll on other living creatures such as members of the deer family (deer, elk, moose); smaller mammals including rodents, raccoons, dogs, and housecats; and birds and insects. Sibley Guides estimate that in North America alone, the lives of 60 million songbirds are extinguished every year by automobiles.

Car owners and drivers apparently accept these deaths as a cost they are willing to pay for the convenience and luxury of getting from point A to point B in their own vehicles.

The Waste of Space and Resources

City planners consider that every automobile requires at least three parking spaces: one at home, one at work, and one at the mall. All of these parking spaces consume valuable land and pave it over using concrete or petroleum-based asphalt, destroying whatever natural habitats originally occupied those sites. Think of how much space is devoted to cars at just your own residence, including the space taken up by carports and garages.

Add to that the cost—financial, environmental, political, and military—of maintaining the flow of petroleum to fuel our cars and pave our roads, as well as the metals and plastics and glass to build the cars.

Pollution

At every stoplight, I sit astride my bicycle and inhale the carbon monoxide, sulfur dioxide, particulate matter, and other poisons being discharged from all the cars around me. I'm not alone, of course; all of the people sitting inside their cars are inhaling the same toxic stew, even if they have their windows closed and the air-conditioning running. In addition, the cars are all spewing the now-notorious carbon dioxide, and we now know what *that* is doing to life on our lovely planet.

Cars pollute not only the air, but water, too. The primary purpose of street-sweepers is not to pick up litter, but to remove some of the toxic effluents from cars (e.g., leaking petrochemicals, brake dust, etc.) that end up on the surface of the street, and to keep those substances from moving into local waterways along with storm water.

Visual Blight

Consider how ugly our otherwise fair cities have become because of the amount of space relegated to the movement, parking, sales, and repair of cars. Look at any urban or suburban street and there are cars everywhere. Most of us accept this as completely normal, but car ownership has been common for less than a century. And although many of us find cars visually attractive, imagine how pleasant your own street would look without parked cars strewn along its curbs and clogging the driveways, and moving cars coming and going constantly.

Noise

Great advances have been made in reducing the amount of noise made by the engines and exhaust pipes of modern automobiles, but even a car with a completely silent engine still generates a great deal of noise—especially at higher speeds—due just to the friction of tires with pavement. And rainy weather accentuates the noise. Where I live, nearly two miles from Interstate 5—the major north-south traffic artery here on the West Coast—even in the middle of the night, I hear the drone of the freeway traffic, most of it from private vehicles.

In addition, car alarms and a variety of noises emitted when one is these days remotely "arming" or "disarming" one's car—from squeaks and warbles to loud horns—add to the cacophony.

Antisocial Behavior

Because most of us travel alone or with just one or two others in the car, we have fewer opportunities to interact with other people in our daily lives. Walking, bicycling, and public transit all bring us into much more contact with each other, instead of separating ourselves from each other by moving around our communities inside our metal and glass boxes.

Many people, when returning to their neighborhoods from work or from errands around town, drive into their driveways, activate remotely the garage door, and disappear inside. They no longer have the opportunity to greet or acknowledge their neighbors as they come and go, and yet another bond to their community is broken.

Cost

There are many other costs associated with car ownership, in addition to those mentioned above to maintain the flow of petroleum to fuel our cars.

Estimates vary, but it's fair to say that the average car owner in the U.S. spends at least several thousand dollars a year for the privilege of driving a private automobile. That includes car payments, insurance, gasoline, registration, and maintenance. Imagine what a wonderful public transit system we would have in this country, were each car owner to pay, say, just half of that sum annually as a transit tax that would improve *everyone's* lives and make our communities truly livable places.

There are many "externalized" costs, too, that are due to private car ownership and that all of us bear in one way or another, from rising sea levels to the loss of natural habitats due to road construction and other paving.

Electric Cars Are Not the Answer

It has been suggested that electric cars will solve our car-related problems and we'll all be able to live happily ever after in a quiet and pollution-free world. But any car, even if it runs on air and produces no harmful emissions, will still contribute to most of the problems mentioned above. Moreover, there are environmental costs to manufacturing, using, and disposing of the batteries which run electric cars—and substantial environmental costs to producing the electricity to recharge the batteries.

If the electricity comes from coal-fired power plants, it just means that the pollution comes out of a big smokestack instead of from your exhaust pipe. And if the source of electricity is a renewable one such as wind or solar, remember that both of those have huge environmental costs themselves, not the least of which is aesthetic, as a landscape covered with wind turbines or solar panels is hardly an attractive addition to the planet—to say nothing of the transmission lines that carry the electricity to cities where it can be used to power electric cars.

Concluding Remarks

Given the costs of privately owned automobiles, I simply cannot comprehend how anyone can justify their use, regardless of their convenience—which is the major reason most people own them in the first place. People want to be able to scoot off to the grocery on a whim to fetch a quart of milk; or take their kids to school instead of letting them walk, bike, or bus there; or leave for work exactly when they want to instead of spending ten or fifteen minutes waiting for and riding the bus; or drive fifty or more miles in order to go for a day hike in the mountains. But these arguably worthwhile reasons do not, to me, justify the clearly nefarious means of attaining them.

And using the private automobile as the standard against which to compare all other transportation options is comparing apples with oranges. *Of course* it's faster and more convenient for you to hop into your car and go to the grocery than it is for you to take a bus or walk. But speed and convenience and personal comfort—as important as they may be to many individuals—should not be the only criteria on which we base our comparison.

The good news is that, as more people have begun to move back to cities—following the flight to suburbia in the latter half of the 20th century—and as other transportation options have improved, Americans are now driving less than they have for many decades, and fewer young Americans than ever are getting driver's licenses and buying cars.

I don't envision a car-free world anytime soon, but I am pleased by the changes we're already seeing in how people get around. And it's exciting to think how much more pleasant our cities—and our lives—may be in the not-so-distant future, as we finally begin to free ourselves from the car culture.

THE INCREDIBLE SHRINKING LANE COUNTY

Far and away the most common response I've heard this past year, when I mention that I'm purposely staying in Lane County for all of 2014, is: "Oh, Lane County is so huge and diverse, you'll have no problem!" The comments are typically made in an almost dismissive manner, as if to suggest that it's no big deal at all to spend an entire year within the county's boundaries. But that's not the point. Even if I still lived in Lancaster County, Pennsylvania, where I grew up—which is less than one-fifth the size of Lane County—I would still have likely chosen that county's borders as my limits, just for convenience.

The *size* of Lane County didn't influence my decision in any way. Rather, I wanted to use a well-defined and recognized boundary, and the county boundary seemed most appropriate. I could have chosen the state's borders, or the city of Eugene's urban growth boundary, or just my own neighborhood. And maybe another year I will choose one of those—but not this year.

How big is Lane County? Well, if I wanted to walk the county's perimeter, which at one point I considered doing during the course of 2014, I would have to walk over 300 miles. And Lane County has an area of 4,722 square miles—almost the size of the state of Connecticut.

Pretty big, eh? But Lane County is today a small fraction of its original size. In 1851, three years after Oregon was formally established as a U.S. Territory—and eight years before statehood—the county's borders were first delineated and the county named. At that time, its northern border extended east some 600 miles, from near present-day Junction City all the way to the continental divide in western Wyoming. Its southern border—

129

about 150 miles from the north border—was the 42nd parallel, south of which lay both the new state of California (created in 1850) and Utah Territory, which at that time included present-day Utah as well as what is now the state of Nevada. Like the northern border, the southern border extended east to the continental divide. That's almost 100,000 square miles. And people think that Lane County is big *these* days!

But the county was to get even bigger. By 1853, Lane County's western border was extended from the west side of the Willamette Valley, up and over the Coast Range to the Pacific Ocean when it took over approximately half of now-defunct Umpqua County—which like Lane was founded in 1851. (By 1862, Umpqua County was eliminated altogether, its northern half having become part of Lane County and its southern half part of Douglas County.)

Then in 1854, Wasco County in the Oregon Territory was created. It included all of the area east of the Cascades—from the Columbia River south to the 42nd parallel, and still extended east to the continental divide. Now *that* was a big county! At the time of Wasco County's creation, Lane County was reduced to its current size by having its eastern border pulled back from Wyoming to the crest of the Cascade Mountains, where it has remained.

JOSH'S REMARK

It's mid-afternoon on Saturday, the last of three days I've spent alone here in the West Cascades, and while I wait for my grilled-cheese sandwich to rest and cool a bit here in the frying pan, I'm thinking again of what Josh said to me just before I left town.

The sun is shining brilliantly now in a deep-blue sky, as it was all day Thursday, my first day up here. Sunshine is certainly lovely and life in the woods is easier on dry days. But wet days are wonderful, too, in their own way, although it's true that they can inconvenience us somewhat, both in town and in the woods. But what's a little inconvenience? Most of us these days lead lives that are even more comfortable than the lives led by European royalty only a century ago. And a little struggle or inconvenience in our lives—a little drama—makes them so much more worthwhile, don't you think? The converse—too much comfort and not enough struggle— can lead to boredom and sloth, just as it did in earlier cultures for many members of the upper classes.

I've never been accused of leading a boring life, and part of the reason is that I have experiences in my everyday life where I am confronted with at least a little discomfort. It could be weather-related, or it might be a setting where I am simply not at ease (e.g., in a noisy restaurant). Perhaps because I have those experiences, the sunny days and peaceful solitude become that much richer and meaningful.

Just what did Josh say? Well, I'd ridden the bus downtown from my neighborhood, and I was carrying a full backpack with tent, sleeping bag, food, and other gear. At the downtown station, where I was waiting to transfer to the bus that would take me up into the Cascades, Josh saw me and came over to say hello. We're good acquaintances, not close friends, who see each other only once a year or so. But I know Josh to be very amicable and respectful, both with me and with others, and he's well suited to his current position as a supervisor of other employees in the company he works for.

We smiled when we saw each other, then shook hands, and Josh asked where I was headed. I told him that I was going to the woods for a few days. And he responded with a smile, "It's s'posed to rain!"

I didn't know quite what to say, as I carefully avoid seeing or hearing weather forecasts, especially before I leave for the woods, as they can create expectations; and besides, the forecasts are not infrequently wrong. So I mumbled something about rain being good, too, and let it go at that. But I've thought more than a few times since then about Josh's remark.

Again, I know Josh to be a pleasant and upbeat kind of guy, not one to purposely say something dismissive or negative. Yet the very first thing he said, when I mentioned I'd be gone for several days, suggested (to me, at least) that I was not likely to have as good a time as I would, were the weather "nicer." I know that he didn't *mean* his comment to be viewed this way, but he made it nonetheless, in the automatic way that so many of us refer to weather.

As a culture, we seem to agree that some weather is "good" and some is "bad." And you're likely to have a better time doing something if it's the former rather than the latter. Unfortunately, that sets all of us up for "good" days and "bad" days, depending on the weather. And because weather—even in Phoenix and San Diego—simply cannot be sunny and 75 degrees *every* day, it suggests that the days of our lives that are less than sunny, and hotter or colder than 75 degrees, will correspondingly be less than pleasant. And that's no way to spend one's short time on the planet, is it?

I'm confident that Josh meant no ill will whatsoever with his remark. But all day Thursday, I kept an eye out for clouds arriving from the west. Would Josh's prediction come to pass? When I went to bed Thursday night, the skies were clear and filled with stars. When I awoke sometime in the night to empty my bladder, however, I noticed that the air felt warmer than it had earlier, and I peeked outside my tent to see that, sure enough, clouds had arrived. Just before dawn, then, there was a brief, heavy shower. When I eventually got up and got dressed to head out for the day, there was already a little sun poking between the clouds. Later Friday morning and off and on through the afternoon, though, brief and light showers fell, so I spent most of my day sitting comfortably beneath my brown tarp lean-to and ended up having a very enjoyable day.

During my second night, there were a couple more very light showers, but when I poked my head out of the tent at dawn this morning, the skies were almost clear above, and to the west it was completely clear. I packed up for the day, fetched water from the little stream just down the hill, and headed off to find a spot to make my breakfast. It's now mid-afternoon and the sun is shining in a cloudless sky.

What rain? Over the course of my three days here, there have been maybe a half-dozen brief showers, all of them between early Friday morning and late Friday night. The rest of the time, it's been sunny. I've had a great time and will be returning to town shortly, revivified by my three days alone in the forest. And I'll still be wondering what Josh meant—if anything—by his remark. Regardless of what he meant, it sure was hard for me to get it out of my mind and just enjoy whatever weather came my way.

AN APPARENTLY COMMON
MISREPRESENTATION
OF LANE COUNTY

Since I've chosen to spend this entire calendar year within the borders of Lane County, I thought it would be interesting to see how the county is portrayed *outside* of its borders. So I looked first where most everyone else looks these days: online, on Wikipedia! I support the idea behind Wikipedia—that anyone can create, update, or delete information about a topic, as long as a reference is provided. On the other hand, I've encountered inaccurate information more than a few times on the website, and I try to steer my students clear of it by telling them that The-Oracle-of-Wikipedia does not know everything.

What turned up when I googled "Lane County" and followed the search results to the Wikipedia site? Not much. The text is quite brief, but it appeared to me to be accurate. What caught my eye, however, were the two images that accompanied the text. One was a photograph of the beautiful but long-gone Lane County Courthouse that stood at the northeast corner of Eighth and Oak from 1898-1959. Why is a building that was demolished more than a half-century ago representing Lane County?

The other image was an oblique aerial view of the central Oregon coast and the Cape Perpetua Visitor Center with the caption, "Cape Perpetua on the coastline of Lane County." Nice photo, but poor caption, as the photo doesn't even include the cape itself—which is just *north* of the visitor center—and both the cape and the visitor center are in Lincoln County, one of three counties (along with Benton and Linn) that lie north of Lane County. Oops.

I'm not very computer-savvy, or I would have immediately attempted to delete that photo, giving the *Atlas of Oregon* as my reference. Instead, I stopped by Travel Lane County—our local tourist information center—on Olive Street in downtown Eugene to tell them about it and, after some friendly conversation with the staff, I was assured that their organization's "web mistress" would look into it.

Not a month later, *Eugene Weekly*—a newspaper distributed for free throughout Lane County and beyond—published the winners of its annual "Best Of" contest: Best Chinese Restaurant, Best Car Mechanic, Best Place to Kiss, and so on. On the page showing the contest results for Best Vacation Spot in Lane County, "Florence and the coast" was number one. A large image accompanying this announcement was, you guessed it, Cape Perpetua.

So I wrote a letter to the editor of the *Eugene Weekly* in which I first acknowledged Americans' deserved reputation for poor geographical knowledge, and then informed the editor and readers that there are plenty of photogenic sites along Lane County's coastline, but Cape Perpetua is not one of them. I suggested that, should a photo be needed in some future issue to represent Lane County's coastline, the paper might use one that shows the picturesque and heavily forested promontory known as Heceta Head, as seen from the remote beach just *north* of it that one reaches via the so-called Hobbit Trail. Heceta Head and its 1894 lighthouse—visible from a pull-out *south* of the headland near Sea Lion Caves—is considered the most photographed site along Oregon's entire coast, and it is admittedly very beautiful. But relatively few people are familiar with the view from the *north*; hence, my suggestion.

Interestingly, while I was speaking with one of the staff at the Travel Lane County office, she acknowledged somewhat embarrassingly that she and her co-workers "often claim Cape Perpetua as a Lane County feature" even though it's a mile or so north of the Lane/Lincoln county line.

Tsk-tsk!

HABITAT LOSS—AND HABITAT GAIN

As our planet's population soars past seven billion and the number of people living in Lane County continues to increase, as well, the amount of land devoted to human needs inevitably increases. For every additional mouth to feed, more land is cleared to raise food—and to build the houses and streets and parking lots to accommodate the other needs of these additional people.

All of this land clearing involves habitat loss, and a diminution of a region's natural flora and fauna. Even when new development takes place on previously developed sites—an agricultural field or a former industrial site, for example—it simply perpetuates the habitat loss that occurred when that site was first devoted to meeting human needs.

Until we are able to rein in our species' population and its ever-increasing demands for food and consumer goods, there is not a lot that we can do about habitat loss caused by the construction of new residential and commercial sites. And increasing the *density* of existing developed areas doesn't address the problem, unless we build *up*. Squeezing more buildings and infrastructure and impervious surfaces into existing developed areas solves nothing, as it just exacerbates the problem by eliminating even more of the already reduced area available for native plants and animals to live within the built environment.

The only real opportunity we have to slow and perhaps eventually reverse habitat loss is to create ecologically functional habitat around both existing and new development. Most contemporary landscape design, however, does just the opposite: it covers the area available for landscaping with static, ecologically dysfunctional swaths of non-native plants, bark mulch, and lawns—all of it requiring irrigation, fertilization, and often the use of pesticides to maintain it—and relegates whatever is left of local biodiversity to parks and preserves.

Natural habitats, whether they occur spontaneously in nature or are thoughtfully re-created, function very differently. Visit any protected natural area or national park and you're sure to see and admire landscapes that are composed exclusively of native plants and animals, and that don't require irrigation, fertilizer, mowing, or the seasonal removal of fallen leaves. These landscapes evolved in place and cost nothing (or very little) to maintain, because nature, when we allow it to work, works for free.

Most people these days understand that a healthy natural environment is essential to human health. Yet, to experience such environments, we have to leave our developed areas and visit special parks or preserves where such functional natural systems are protected and permitted to carry on, just as they have since time immemorial. But it doesn't have to be that way. We know how to integrate such biologically diverse landscapes right where we live. It's just that the dysfunctional alternative has become so omnipresent, that few people even know anymore what an area's "natural" landscape looks like.

There are very few constructed landscapes here in the Upper Willamette Valley that include appropriate natural habitats—that is, native grasslands, savannas, or woodlands. Far and away the best example is a site that most people would consider a very unlikely candidate for such landscaping: the Roosevelt Operations Center (ROC) of the Eugene Water and Electric Board (EWEB). EWEB decided to build its new operations center on a historically abused industrial site in west Eugene. But instead of continuing the abuse by building a conventional building and surrounding it with a conventional and dysfunctional landscape, it chose instead to create one of the most thoughtfully designed and environmentally friendly industrial sites in the entire state of Oregon.

As remarkable as the building itself is, it's the new landscape surrounding it that truly merits attention. Instead of scraping the site bare, then hauling in truckloads of loam and thousands of non-native plants to create a landscape that *gives* virtually nothing and *takes* a lot of money, time, and materials to maintain it—from fossil fuel and bark mulch, to water and pesticides—the new landscape is a simply superb re-creation of both wetland and upland habitats that might have at one time naturally occurred on the site.

Storm water from paved areas and building roofs moves through the site's restored wetlands and eventually out into the huge and wildlife-rich West Eugene Wetlands complex. All of the plants used in the landscape surrounding the building are native to this part of the Willamette Valley and, except for some supplemental watering during their establishment period, require no long-term irrigation. It's only appropriate that our local utility should set an example for water *conservation*. But it's equally important that the utility should demonstrate, as it does so well, the need for maintaining water *quality* by treating its storm water—as the water moves slowly through the new wetlands, where the plants filter out any impurities—before the water leaves the site.

Most important of all, however, is that by re-creating an ecologically functional landscape—instead of doing business-as-usual by imposing a collection of non-native plants on the site—our entire community benefits from the "habitat gain."

Each time I visit the site with my students, we're delighted to see reminders that EWEB did the right thing. This past October, as we entered the parking lot, a flock of western meadowlarks took flight from the restored grassland. In this part of Oregon, populations of our state bird are threatened due to the loss of appropriate grassland habitat. So by providing biologically diverse grassland, instead of a huge expanse of mowed lawn, EWEB is helping the meadowlarks, as well as countless other inhabitants, both plants and animals, that need this type of habitat.

Some of EWEB's ratepayers have complained that too much money was spent on both the building and its restored landscape. But the ROC facility came in $11 million *under*-budget and resulted in a rate increase of less than three percent spread out over three years. That's already a substantial savings. And if one looks closely at what the site "takes" for its long-term care—relatively little water, fossil fuel, and electricity—and what it "gives" in terms of healthy, functional habitat, there is little question that we ratepayers are already benefitting and will continue to benefit in a variety of ways from the EWEB board's thoughtful investment.

The ROC site is apparently the first industrial building in Oregon to earn gold-level LEED (Leadership in Energy and Environmental Design) certification, and the landscape restoration that it elected to do is likely what bumped it up from LEED's silver level to gold. EWEB has created a site that we all can be proud of. It is a shining example of how every property—residential, commercial, and industrial—could look and function now and in the future.

A CHANGE OF AIR, A CHANGE OF ATTITUDE

The bus ride up into the Cascades today was particularly unpleasant. Once again, in a brand-new bus, exhaust instead of fresh air was being pumped into the passenger compartment. This happens on a fairly regular basis and I cannot help but wonder why. Since it's been well over a century since internal combustion engines were first used to propel enclosed vehicles, one would think that engineers and mechanics had by now figured out how to vent exhaust *outside* the vehicle, and bring fresh air *into* the vehicle. But perhaps I've set my expectations too high.

It was with considerable relief, then, that I arrived at my stop, shouldered my pack, grabbed my hiking stick, and exited the bus into the fresh mountain air. There's nothing like a lungful of West Cascades air, clean as a whistle and fragrant with the scent of conifer needles. It was delightful to be able to take deep breaths again after all of my "shallow" breathing on the bus—where all of the windows are sealed shut—in a failed effort to limit the amount of toxins I had to inhale from the engine exhaust.

Although it had been raining hard when I left Eugene and my rain gauge in town measured nearly an inch of rain since yesterday afternoon, the woods were relatively dry. So I started out wearing only my rubber boots, and kept my rain pants tidily folded inside my pack. The air was unseasonably mild—in the mid-50s, as it has been the past few days back in town—and there wasn't a breath of wind. I felt great!

Less than a mile from the bus stop, as I was walking up the forest road to the area where I planned to spend the day, I was startled by a whooshing sound. I looked into the upper canopy of the adjacent forest to see the treetops waving back and forth. How bizarre, as it was absolutely calm down where I was walking.

Before I knew what was happening, I was enveloped in a giant bubble of incredibly warm air, easily in the upper 60s and maybe even the low 70s. I'd taken only one big gulp when the bubble moved on and the temperature was back in the mid-50s. But what a wonderful treat! I don't know where the bubble came from or went to, and right after its departure, the tree canopy was still once again.

I've experienced a similar phenomenon back in the Willamette Valley where, after several consecutive days of cold, dank fog during a winter temperature inversion, a new air mass arrives from the Pacific along with the wind that's pushing it across the Coast Range and into the Willamette Valley. Little by little, the wind sweeps the cold fog away and replaces it with warm air that is fragrant with the conifers of the Coast Range, through whose canopies it has passed on its way to the Willamette Valley.

After I'd inhaled the warm fragrant air earlier this morning, I was reminded of a winter day in the mid-1990s when I was bicycling into town during an extended temperature inversion. Just as I was passing through the Owen Rose Garden on the riverside bike path, my cheeks were suddenly caressed by another bubble of warm, balmy air that was just arriving from the ocean and was beginning to "poke holes" in the fog layer.

As I continued along the bike path, I quickly entered the cold fog again. But over the course of the next hour or so, *all* of the cold fog was replaced by the fresh, warm air, and the crocuses that had been shivering for days in the cold, opened their petals wide in the warm sunshine.

That's how I felt this morning. I wasn't in the best of moods after the unpleasant bus ride, but when I was briefly bathed in the bubble of exceedingly warm and fragrant air, I opened the petals of my heart to the loveliness of the day ahead of me. And I've felt wonderful ever since.

THE WIND THAT WASN'T

While riding the inbound bus to Eugene Station, where I would transfer to the bus that would take me to the West Cascades for the day, one of my bus mates expressed concern for my personal safety because of "the strong windstorm" that, according to him, was forecast for later in the day. To reinforce the gravity of the situation, he mentioned that a good friend of his who's very comfortable in the out-of-doors and is an avid wild mushroom harvester, had actually chosen to remain in town today rather than risk his life by venturing out into the woods.

I'm accustomed to this ongoing commentary about weather and weather forecasts that is so prevalent in our culture, although I make every effort myself to avoid forecasts and instead prefer simply to "live in the moment." I'm not sure what good it does anyway, to anticipate something that might never develop—as forecasts, at least here in the Northwest, are often wrong.

But I also acknowledge that, for some people, this "weather-tainment" is an important part of their lives. Several years ago, when I visited an aging aunt and her boyfriend at their home in Wisconsin, I was both amazed and amused at how many hours they spent daily watching the Weather Channel. What on earth difference does it make if Topeka, Kansas is getting lightning strikes at the rate of one per minute, or if the Deep South is having unseasonably cold temperatures, when one lives in Wisconsin? I eventually realized, however, that their watching the Weather Channel brought some excitement, albeit vicarious, into their lives. Want some drama in your humdrum life? Just turn on the television!

My bus-ride into the Cascades was uneventful—and no one else expressed concern over my safety, in light of the high wind warning. But once I arrived at the ranger station where I had a brief errand, the subject of the weather returned and I was in for more admonition. The receptionist— who knows me and knew I would be spending my day outside in the woods, where big trees might fall down in a windstorm—asked me if I was aware of the chance I was taking by going off alone into big timber, when unusually high winds were predicted. I smiled and thanked her for her concern, and assured her that I would take every precaution to avoid falling branches and trees, and then I headed down the trail.

The forenoon was wonderfully mild and absolutely calm as I sat at the base of a 450-year-old Douglas-fir and ate my breakfast, then wrote a little and took a nap. Midday, I hiked a little farther up the hill, just to get some exercise and see a different part of the woods. Early in the afternoon, a strong gust of wind suddenly came up from the west, and the conifers' tops all pointed sideways. "Oh, goody—here comes the wind!" I thought. Things calmed down again. There was a second gust a few minutes later, but after that it was quiet.

The rest of the afternoon, just like the forenoon, was unseasonably mild and absolutely calm, without a breath of air. And I thought about next week, when I see my commuting buddy again, and I get to tell him about the wind that wasn't. I'll ask that he give my condolences to his mushroom-hunting friend who ended up spending his day in town, for naught.

STEVIE'S QUESTION

Several years ago, I decided to stop giving exams in my university courses. That's right: no more midterms, no more finals. As much as I enjoyed writing the exams, I never liked giving them, knowing as I did how much stress it creates for my students. The stress was not short-lived. There was pre-exam stress, mid-exam stress, and post-exam stress. The principal problem was that almost all of my students really enjoyed my courses, but they invariably did poorly on my exams—and that just didn't feel right to them or to me.

So for the past few years, I've given my students multiple quizzes during the course of the ten-week term, a couple of at-home essays to write, and a term project to complete. These assignments keep them engaged and comparatively unstressed while providing for me at least something on which to base their grades. Then, during finals week, we have a final class meeting—and maybe the last quiz—but there's no crushing exam to face. Instead, we have a little party, and part ways on a happy note instead of a sad one.

I always bake something—this fall, it was persimmon cake with cream-cheese frosting. And I show a few of my fun little videos for some last laughs. And I usually provide some end-of-the-term gifts for my teaching assistants as well as the students.

For the past two years in my fall course, The Nature of Eugene, I've given each student a handsome card with a color photograph of the university's oldest building, Deady Hall—completed in 1876—that was taken after one of Eugene's rare snowfalls. The towers of the lovely so-called Second Empire-style building are silhouetted against a deep blue sky, and the huge, old conifers surrounding the building are all bedecked with snow. I also

143

include a stamped envelope with each card. And I remind my students that almost everyone loves getting first-class mail—even though few people these days send any—and I want them to write just a few lines on the card and send it to their parents.

It's finals week and they're under a lot of strain, at least in their other courses, and most of them will be headed home soon for the holiday break. So just saying, "Dear Mom and Dad, It looks like I'm going to survive my finals, and I can't wait to see you next week! Love, so-and-so," will mean a lot. I know for a fact that almost all of the students complete and send their cards. They really *like* the idea of doing it, even though they would be very unlikely to take the time themselves to buy a card and an envelope and a stamp. Providing for them everything they need—including a suggestion of what to say—makes it just so easy.

I know, too, of course, that they're not at all accustomed to writing and sending what I call *real* mail (as opposed to e-mail). I was reminded of that fact during our last class meeting this fall. After the videos and the cake and apple juice, students were leaving singly and in small groups, almost all of them coming up to me to say thank you for the class before walking out the door. When about half the class had already left, Stevie came up to me, holding his completed and sealed envelope, and asked me, "What do I do with it now?" I cheerfully responded, "Just mail it!" And Stevie asked, "Where?"

Suddenly, I realized that Stevie had never mailed a letter before and needed direction. I started to explain about the big blue metal boxes on four legs, with rounded tops, and was going to direct him to the one on central campus, not far from our classroom. Then I just said, "I'll mail it for you, Stevie." And we parted.

Wow. Only later that evening while having my dinner—after all the hubbub of the last day of class—did it really hit me that well-mannered, intelligent, 22-year-old Stevie had never mailed a letter before. How could that be? And then I thought of my own middle-aged peers, many of whom these days use only Facebook and e-mail and Twitter and whatever other novelty to communicate. Real mail is headed very fast for the ash heap of history, and the generations to come will have no idea whatsoever of what they missed out on.

It was a stunning reminder of just how wide the chasm already is between my generation and today's youth—and how rapidly the chasm continues to widen. Probably since the dawn of civilization, there have been intergenerational differences. It's just that since the Industrial Revolution, the pace of technological changes has picked up so dramatically that it's become increasingly easy to be just left behind in the dust.

THE BENCH

Passersby sometimes mistake my property for a public park. When I've on occasion had the opportunity to ask a visitor what it is about my yard that prompts that response, some of them refer to the lot's attractive landscape—in contrast to several less well-kept neighbors' properties—and others point to the "Welcome" sign at the base of the boardwalk ramp that leads upslope into the front yard. But usually, the visitors refer to the cedar bench located not ten feet into my property from the public sidewalk.

It's a simple enough bench made out of western redcedar. Because I do in fact welcome the public onto my property, I wanted a place where visitors could feel comfortable sitting down and just resting, or enjoying the landscape which I've created. The bench of course had to be visible from the public sidewalk, so passersby know it's there, and it also had to be far enough from the sidewalk and surrounded with enough vegetation to afford some privacy from the public realm of the street and sidewalk. Likewise, it had to be far enough from the house so visitors don't feel they're either intruding on, or being watched by, the residents.

I'm very particular about benches, most of which I find rather uncomfortable due to their poor design. But one fall, when I was teaching a field class in the redwood forests of coastal northern California, I came upon a trailside bench that was just perfect. It was carved out of a redwood log perhaps three feet in diameter—as if about one quarter of the log, in the longitudinal sense, had been removed, creating a flat area for sitting and a flat back to lean against. The bench was so simple and so strikingly comfortable that I took some notes of its angles: the angle from the horizontal at which the seat was tilted; the angle from the vertical at which the back was tilted; and then the angle between the back and the seat itself, which was a little more than 90 degrees.

Later, back in Eugene, when I had both the time and the money, I hired a carpenter to build for me the perfect bench according to the specifications I'd noted in Jedediah Smith Redwoods State Park, just east of Crescent City, California. Using two short planks of scrap wood and several adjustable clamps, my carpenter made a bench mock-up for me to try out. We then played with the angles of both the seat and the back until I thought it was a perfect replica of the redwood-log bench I'd fallen in love with. Then he got to work constructing this important addition to my front yard.

The bench was installed, appropriately enough, beneath a towering, two-trunked coast redwood tree at the entrance to my property that shaded much of the front yard. Even on a hot summer day, the redwood's deep shade and low-hanging branches afforded a relatively cool and fairly secluded spot to rest. And, over the years, I caught glimpses now and again—from inside my house or somewhere out in the yard—of visitors using the bench.

More than a few times, I saw a young mother nursing her infant in the restful spot I'd created there beneath the redwood. And I once observed two little girls—on their way home from the nearby elementary school—sitting on the bench and talking animatedly about the things that matter to little girls.

One especially warm August day, I returned home from campus, and as I walked my bike up the boardwalk ramp into the welcome shade, I was surprised to see a young man stretched out and asleep on the bench. He was not very well groomed, and a large disheveled backpack lay on the ground nearby. I don't think he had a place to call home, but he'd found a pleasant temporary home on the cedar bench. I didn't bother him, but instead just quietly wheeled my bike past him, on my way up to the house. Later that afternoon, when I went back outside, he was gone.

Seeing these visitors—and many others over the years—reminds me on a regular basis that my bench, as costly as it was to have built in the first place, has repaid me many times over with the heartwarming scenes I've witnessed. But the most touching scene I've ever observed at the bench occurred this past spring, on the first day of April.

Because I had to remove the lovely redwood tree several years ago, the bench is now somewhat more exposed to the public eye—and to my eyes, as well, from the upstairs loft of my house where my desk faces a window that looks out over the front yard. But I tried to compensate for the loss of the tree and the privacy its dense canopy afforded by building an attractive wooden arbor over the bench and the small brick terrace adjacent to it, and planting vines and small trees nearby. So passersby continue to be attracted to the bench now for very much the same reasons they were drawn to it when the redwood still stood.

I'd been working on a project at my desk for much of the lovely spring afternoon, occasionally raising my head from my work to just gaze outside toward the distant hills, or into the tops of the young trees in the front yard. I hadn't noticed anyone at the bench, and I certainly don't *watch* the bench per se from my "observation tower" in the loft, yet I can't help but notice sometimes when visitors arrive, especially if I can hear their voices.

This particular afternoon, I glanced out at one point and saw that a young couple had arrived and were sitting on the bench. They looked to be in their late teens or early twenties. When I first noticed them, they were sitting side-by-side and not touching each other. The young woman sat with her head upright and was looking straight ahead. She was evidently talking to the young man at her side who sat with his head deeply bowed, his chin almost on his chest. Evidently, some small or large tragedy had occurred, and the young man might even have been weeping. But I didn't think that much of it, and of course didn't want to intrude on their privacy, so I concentrated once again on my work.

The next time I looked out the window, maybe five or ten minutes later, the young man had straightened up, but I could see from the look on his face that he continued to be distraught. The young woman had reached over to him with her left hand and was toying with the hair on the back of the young man's head. I smiled, but was a little teary-eyed myself at what I was witnessing.

After a few more minutes of deskwork, I looked outside once more, not quite as absentmindedly as I had the first two times. Now, her head was leaning on his right shoulder, and his head was leaning against hers.

More deskwork. The fourth and last time I looked out, I smiled broadly to see that the young man's girlfriend (evidently) was sitting on his lap and they had their arms around each other. I wanted to believe that whatever difficulty there had been, had now been resolved—or at least discussed amicably—during the half-hour or so that they'd spent on the bench.

My fourth glance out the window was as brief as the other three had been. Each time, I just happened to note changes since the previous glance, then got back to minding my own business. Sometime later, when I looked out one more time, the young couple had already departed.

I seldom sit on my own bench. But knowing the role it's played over the past fifteen years in the lives of countless visitors—most of whom I did not happen to see—brings me a great deal of joy. The bench that I designed with my own personal comfort in mind has, in the end, provided comfort to many others in a variety of ways. It's been a very worthwhile investment.

CHRISTMAS EVE AT THE BORDER

Although the rain let up in the past hour or so, it was a very wet forenoon and I brought along my tarp so that, even if the rain had continued, I could still picnic here in relative comfort. In just the past few minutes, however, the cloud cover has thinned enough to reveal the location of the sun. So I've decided to sit facing that direction and be ready to soak up its warmth if the clouds do decide to part.

By chance, someone recently tossed some Douglas-fir branches along the side of the road here, so I've broken off a dozen small pieces and made a pile of them just ten feet or so from the pavement, then placed my blue foam sit-upon atop the fragrant boughs. It's a very comfortable seat.

In front of me is a thicket of Himalayan blackberries, at the corner of which is a cluster of three trees: two 50-foot-tall bigleaf maples and a strangely sinuous valley ponderosa pine with multiple tops that emerge just above the maples' canopies. Evidently, the pine had a troubled youth growing among the faster-growing maples, but its head is now out in the sunshine and it looks like it's going to win this race for the sky after all.

Just south of the blackberry thicket is an abandoned and decrepit farm out-building set among some century-old Oregon white oaks. But there's so much trash around it that I have no desire whatsoever to try to get a peek inside the old building.

The landscape is otherwise wide-open—typical of the middle of the Willamette Valley. The crops growing here, too, include the usual suspects. To the southwest is a field of sugar beets, likely being grown for their seed, which will mature in the plants' second year in the ground. (Beets are biennials, or plants that make just green leaves their first year, then flower and set seed and die the second.) To the northeast is an orchard of young filberts (or hazelnuts) that can't be even ten years old. And both southeast and northwest of me are grass-seed fields.

I arrived midday, having caught the 11:30 bus to Junction City from Eugene, and then pedaled here from the Lindeborg stop in central Junction City—which, although it is incorporated as a bona fide city, is really only a *town* with a population of just over 5,000. Leaving town and heading north, I had to ride along Highway 99E for less than a mile, but even that short distance was very unpleasant due to the lack of a bike lane, the continuing rain, and the traffic speeding by me at barely arm's length. Thankfully, I was able to leave the noisy, frightening highway at Link Road, a refreshingly quiet rural road that led me here—Noraton Road—via Toftdahl and Howard roads.

The area is mostly agricultural, thanks to the deep, fertile, well-drained loam brought here over the millennia by the wandering Willamette, as it moved back and forth across its very broad floodplain. The scattered houses are a mix of *charming*, small, older frame houses—mostly abandoned or ill-maintained—and *charmless*, much larger and newer houses which have been imposed on this rural landscape in just the past decade or so.

Soon after turning onto Link Road, I scared up a snipe from the wet roadside ditch; I don't see them very often. I saw several kestrels on my way here, sitting solitarily on the roadside utility wires. And just before reaching Noraton Road, I passed nearly directly beneath a red-tailed hawk that was sitting high in a large cottonwood tree and watching me.

Since arriving here at my picnic spot, I've heard some robin squabbles, seen several scrub jays, and am now listening to European starlings singing nearby. As expected on a late December day in this area, flock after flock of Canada geese can be seen and heard as they fly from one field to another in search of a meal before retiring to Fern Ridge Reservoir southwest of here, where they will spend the night on the open water.

Over the past year, I've visited five different spots along Lane County's border where I could peer into the neighboring counties—Lincoln, Douglas, Deschutes, Klamath, and Linn. But I hadn't yet said hello to our sixth neighbor, Benton County, so that's what brought me here on Christmas Eve. My bicycle a few feet away from me is in fact leaning against a sturdy six-by-six wooden post on which the word LANE is engraved vertically on one face, and the word COUNTY on the other.

When parking my bike, I poked my head briefly into the neighboring county to the north, and the other two faces of the post say—no surprise—BENTON and COUNTY. I've not seen a post like this at any of the other border crossings I've visited. It's a very nice touch.

In addition, attached to a taller, galvanized-metal post is a large sign facing south (i.e., toward me) that says, "At Your Service Every Day." A little drawing in the corner of the sign says "Benton County Oregon" and includes a sketch of the lovely, Italianate, nineteenth-century Benton County courthouse in downtown Corvallis, the county seat. Coming from the *north*, one encounters a sign facing that direction that says: "Lane County—Enjoy Our County Roads." I've been amused at every border crossing I've visited this year, to see how each county portrays itself in its welcome sign.

Besides birds, some of the other sounds I've heard since arriving here include a large commercial jet somewhere above the clouds; a truck using its compression brakes on Highway 99W just a little more than a mile west of me; the muffled blasts of a train horn about three miles east of here on the Union Pacific tracks; the omnipresent and always unwanted (by some of us) screech of a back-up beeper; and of course the occasional motorized vehicle along little-used Noraton Road—mostly relatively quiet cars, but also some incredibly loud diesel pickups.

As mentioned above, the view from mid-valley here is an expansive one. To the west is the Coast Range, where I've had fleeting glimpses of snow-covered ridges as the clouds come and go. And to the east, more snow-covered hills—in this case, the Coburg Hills, which are part of the West Cascades. It's not very often that the snow level is this low in winter, so when it happens, it's always a visual treat. In fact, early this morning back in Eugene, the rain was initially mixed with big fat flakes of snow, as the temperature was only in the high 30s. This is a big change after more than a week of unseasonably mild weather with temperatures in the upper 50s some days.

One of the striking features of this site is the incredible lack of biodiversity. Sure, it's agricultural land, with monocultures of, in this case, beets, grass, and filberts. But until quite recently, farmers' fields were divided by hedgerows of mostly native shrubs, small trees, wildflowers, and grasses. And along roadsides, a combination of native and non-native plants could be found. These areas were important habitat for a variety of now-rare wildflowers as well as songbirds, insects, and other creatures such as reptiles, amphibians, and small mammals. But over the past decade or two, changing agricultural practices—especially the increased use of herbicides—have led to the almost complete elimination of these remnant biotic communities that had already been reduced to a tiny fraction of their original extent in this great interior valley of western Oregon.

One of the most heartbreaking examples of this loss of biodiversity is the recent near-extirpation of our native showy milkweed (*Asclepias speciosa*). The plant itself is a fascinating one with its three-foot-tall stems bearing large oval leaves which, when broken, ooze a milky latex or sap. And the plant's fragrant pink flowers are borne in spherical clusters two or three inches across. Milkweed is the host plant for monarch butterflies, which will lay their eggs *only* on milkweed plants. The western population of monarchs here in North America is, like the much more populous eastern race, in dire trouble due in part to the disappearance of its host plant. The Willamette Valley plays a crucial role for the butterflies when they head north in spring from their over-wintering areas along the central California coast. The monarchs that survived the winter migrate north through the Siskiyou Mountains of southwesternmost Oregon, where they lay their eggs there on native milkweed plants and then die. A second generation of monarchs then continues the journey northward. But when those monarchs reach the Willamette Valley, their host plant is increasingly difficult to find, and the population risks disappearing completely if this vital link in the chain of milkweed sources is broken.

There are certainly other organisms whose populations are threatened by these new agricultural practices, as well. My point is that since Euro-Americans arrived here in the valley and brought with them their agriculture, there has always been at least some available habitat for the remaining native plants and animals, either in hedgerows or along field and roadside edges. But now that those last refuges are disappearing in front of the herbicide applicators' nozzles, we risk losing the already very limited remains of this area's once-rich natural diversity.

Another flock of Canada geese flying overhead towards Fern Ridge reminds me that, although this twenty-fourth day of December is already a little bit longer than the winter solstice was a few days ago, it's still mighty short. So I should be moving along, in order to get back to Junction City and Eugene before dark.

As always, I've had an interesting hour or so just sitting here at the border, eating my picnic lunch, observing my surroundings, and reflecting on the site's existing landscape.

EPILOGUE

After leaving my lunch spot where the Lane-Benton county line crosses Noraton Road, I decided to visit the next border crossing to the west—namely the one along Highway 99W. I really dreaded biking along another stretch of busy highway again, but my mood was good, thanks to the brilliant sunshine I had enjoyed for a while.

Along the way, just north of the junction of Jaeger Road and 99W, I passed the long-gone site of Othello—which doesn't even show up on contemporary maps, but is shown on the 1960s-era map I prefer to use for my rural adventures. According to McArthur's *Oregon Geographic Names*, Othello actually had a post office between 1855 and 1859.

When I arrived at what my map calls Washburne State Wayside—a grove of tall Douglas-fir trees on the east side of the highway, right at the border crossing—I was disappointed to find nothing but a parking area, and a dated monument recognizing Highway 99W as a "Blue Star Highway." I recall that, during my grad school days in Corvallis in the late 1970s, this area had picnic tables and a restroom. Now, there's not even a sign saying that it's a state wayside. While wandering around among the tall firs, I noticed car after car pull into the former wayside parking lot. No one got out of any of the vehicles, and none of them stayed more than a few minutes before moving on. What were they doing? Pulling over to read or send text messages? Somehow, I doubt it.

My map suggested that, across the road, there was more public land called Benton Lane Park. But to me, it looked like someone's front yard. What happened?

Something that considerably detracted from my otherwise pleasant visit to the wayside area was the stench of cow manure blowing in on the south wind from a huge dairy operation less than a mile away. I'd thought of having my afternoon snack in the fir grove, but changed my mind because of the strong smell.

Anyway, it was time to head back south on 99W to Lingo Lane, then Toftdahl, and back to Junction City to catch the late-afternoon bus and return to Eugene. I'd had a mostly pleasant day exploring a part of Lane County about which I had known very little before. And, as attractive as Benton County appeared from my picnic spot, I decided I'd just as soon stay in Lane County a little while longer before venturing beyond its borders once again.

A TROUBLING PEEK AT OUR CORRECTIONS SYSTEM

In mid-February, I received a letter in the mail that was stamped on the back side: INMATE'S MAIL—Lane County Adult Corrections. On the front of the envelope, both my address and the return address were written in pencil, and in lovely cursive. I didn't immediately recognize the name of the sender, but after opening the letter, I realized it was from a former student of mine—whom I'll refer to here as Chad.

Chad had been able to attend only the first few films of my winter term *Nordic Film Series* on campus before being whisked away to jail. He explained in his letter that he'd decided to write to me based in part on his intuition—that I'd be a reliable correspondent during his incarceration— and in part on comments I'd made about the humane and respectful treatment of inmates in Denmark, where one of the films I'd shown was set. Before showing *"In Your Hands"* (*Forbrydelser* in Danish), I'd compared the U.S. and Danish corrections systems based on a half-dozen criteria, from general living conditions, to length of stay and average rate of recidivism. On all counts, the Danish system was far superior to the U.S. system. Perhaps the most significant difference was the Danish correction system's focus on rehabilitating inmates so that they can re-enter society as productive, rather than destructive, participants.

So began our correspondence by mail that lasted for several weeks, during which time the letters sometimes just flew back and forth. Over that period of time, I received eight letters from Chad, and he received a similar number from me. We discussed a great variety of topics in our letters, from the reason for his incarceration—a neighborhood dispute that frankly should not have led to this young man going to jail—and the *Nordic Film Series*, to jail food and stories from Chad's past. All of Chad's letters were written in pencil and, as I said earlier, were in beautiful cursive, which is so rare these days. It turns out that Chad was not permitted to have a pen— which, I was told, might be used as a weapon or to self-inflict harm. He was allowed to use only what he called "golf pencils," which were just a few inches long. More than once, he remarked about how painful it was to write his long letters with such short pencils. And because he wrote only in pencil, he referred to me in his letters as his "pencil pal" rather than the more conventional pen pal.

Since I had no idea what the view from Chad's cell was like, I asked him to draw me a sketch of it. A few days later, when I received his return letter that included the sketch, I was absolutely astonished at his artistic skill. I recognized the Down-to-Earth building in the foreground of course, but Chad had also painstakingly included every large tree that was visible from his cell, as he knew that I teach "the trees class" at the university and would likely recognize my "friends." Indeed, there was one of my favorite sequoias on the west side of the Parcade parking garage, as well as the northern red oaks that line West Sixth Avenue.

When I asked him for more details about his cell, Chad sent me a second sketch—this time, of the interior of his cell—which was even more phenomenal than the first. I could see the *Nordic Film Series* poster I'd sent him at his request and that he'd taped to his wall, every book on his little bookshelf, the roll of toilet paper by the cell's toilet, and much more.

In the meantime, I decided to visit Chad at the jail—my very first visit to a jail—as he'd written to me when the visiting times were. I showed up one weekday afternoon, anticipating seeing him. He'd already been in jail for more than a week and, according to his letters, he had had no visitors. Immediately upon entering the jail, I found the interior to be dark and uninviting, which seemed to me inappropriate—if in fact the "mission" of the jail was to rehabilitate ("correct") and eventually return the inmates to society as improved versions of their former selves.

I ascended the stairs to speak with the jail attendant, who turned out to be very cool and even a bit surly toward me. He almost reluctantly acknowledged that Chad was an inmate there—it's no secret, as information about all the inmates was, to my utter surprise, available online—and said that Chad couldn't have any visitors unless he'd provided the jail ahead of time with the proper request form on which he had written the visitor's name, address, and birth date. Of course, Chad couldn't have known my birth date, so I made sure in my next letter to him that I included that information. I was not allowed to leave a note for him with the attendant, as "the rules" state that all communication with inmates must be by first class U.S. mail.

After leaving the cold, stark building that afternoon, I took the time to bicycle around the west and north sides of the jail, just to look more closely at the building, and I was disappointed to see chainlink fences topped with razor-wire. I understand the need to confine the inmates to the jail property, but there are other ways to achieve that end without making the place look like a nineteenth-century asylum.

Over the next couple of weeks, Chad made several more unsuccessful attempts to have me cleared for a visit. Eventually, I was given approval— but by that time, Chad had been released. So I never got to visit him in jail. Moreover, according to the rules, once an inmate has submitted a form for a visitor, he cannot change or add anyone else to the list for *three weeks*. The reason for this rule is not clear.

My communication with Chad was thwarted in other ways, as well. During what Chad called his "all-expenses-paid vacation downtown," he was allowed to make telephone calls during his two-hour-long day-room visits. But he could place only collect calls, and because the times of his day-room visits varied from one day to the next, I couldn't be sure when he might call. I don't use a mobile phone, so I needed to be near my home phone when he called. Alas, most times he tried to call, he spoke only with my voicemail. And I was not permitted to call Chad; he had to call me.

On top of all the aforementioned, Chad eventually had his two-hour day-room privileges taken away because of a "mail violation" that he didn't even commit. It turned out that a just-minted young deputy was simply taking the opportunity afforded by his badge to exercise control over someone (Chad) who didn't always bow down to the deputy's authority.

Chad wasn't the only partner in our correspondence who had a long list of rules to abide by—some of them simply incomprehensible. I too had to be extremely careful about what I included in my care packages (my mail) to him. Here is a partial list of items that I was prohibited from sending to Chad: "newspaper and magazine clippings; drawings made with crayon, colored pencils or other types of art medium; paper clips; postage stamps; envelopes; blank writing paper or cards; and unofficial or decorative ink stampings." I'm proud to say that I illegally (!) stamped the back of almost every one of my letters to Chad with a rubber stamp I designed years ago that says simply: "Letters Lift Spirits." All of that mail somehow slipped by the inspector.

In one of his early letters, Chad revealed that this wasn't his first visit to the Lane County jail. He'd even been in the state prison briefly. As far as I could tell, all of these "vacations" were due to behavioral difficulties Chad sometimes has due to a mental disability. Despite his history of multiple and usually brief periods of incarceration, he maintained an ever-hopeful and cheerful attitude while in jail. And because he saw me too as a cheerful and optimistic person, his letters were long and heartfelt, and full of revealing stories about himself and his upbringing in comparatively privileged circumstances in California.

At my urging, Chad was forthright in his letters with his analysis of the corrections system's shortcomings, which appear to be many. Foremost among them is the treatment that inmates receive while incarcerated. Quoting Chad, "The district attorney's best weapon in winning cases is making the [inmate] so miserable and exasperated that [he] will accept an unfair deal, simply to get out of this unjust situation." From two of my other young students who have also gotten in trouble with the law—for very minor offenses—I know this to be true. Both of these other students, in unrelated cases, had to accept a plea bargain in which they acknowledged doing something that they had *not* done, in order to receive a lesser punishment. In other words, they had to lie. Is this what our corrections system should be teaching people?

As far as I could tell, none of Chad's letters to me was censored in any way. And to ensure that we were indeed receiving every letter that we sent to each other, I decided to number mine so Chad would know if any letter in the sequence was missing. Apparently, they all got through—and that's as it should be.

But there were other aspects of Chad's confinement that I found troubling. Yes, he was accused of doing something unlawful, and until his case was resolved, he was denied the liberty to move around at will in his community. That, from my perspective, is punishment enough. For Chad—and other inmates, presumably—to be subjected to a host of other indignities, to put it mildly, is, from my point of view, inhumane and completely uncalled-for.

Making Chad's communication with the outside world difficult was bad enough. But in addition, the food was, in a word, inedible. When an inmate rejoices over being given institution-style oatmeal for breakfast—as

Chad did more than once—you can't help but wonder what the other menu options were.

No, I don't believe inmates should be rewarded for their misdeeds and live in posh quarters. But they should be assured a reasonably decent quality of life while incarcerated. This would include some freedom of movement within the building. Chad was more than once confined to his cell and not even allowed to shower. As far as I know, he was not once permitted to go outdoors. Yes, there were windows in his cell, but they were long, horizontal slits near the top of the wall, so to do his sketch of the view from his cell, Chad had to stand on top of his bed. And the windows couldn't be opened, so he had no access to fresh air—only that air which came in through the building's ventilation system.

Add to all of this the mistreatment he suffered at the hands of more than one deputy—treatment which at best might be called demeaning—and an outsider cannot help but feel troubled by the inferior living conditions of our jail. Yet Chad never complained to me about any of these issues. Rather, he accepted them and simply answered the questions I asked him in my letters.

The best hope we have for "correcting" anyone's behavior is by modeling more appropriate behavior ourselves, be that in the outside world or inside our penal institutions. Many of those who are incarcerated grew up under unpleasant circumstances where they were abused or otherwise treated disrespectfully. To further abuse and disrespect them as inmates achieves nothing; it only hardens them more to the world around them.

I'm embarrassed beyond words by what I've experienced myself and what I've learned through Chad about life behind bars in my own county's jail. To suggest that our jail—or any other penal institution in the U.S.—is part of a "corrections" system stretches credulity. The word *corrections* implies that some sort of rehabilitation goes on before inmates are released back into society. But from what I've seen and heard, the word "revenge" better describes our system. "You did a bad thing, so now we're going to treat you badly."

The approach to the treatment of prisoners in Europe's Nordic countries (e.g., Denmark and Norway) is almost the polar opposite of this, and likely the reason those countries have been so much more successful in remolding the lives of their inmates. There, from what I have learned, they generally treat inmates respectfully in an effort to retrain them so they won't make the same mistake again. Eventually, then, when they're released back into society, they'll be able to lead productive and satisfying lives as respectful and respected members of their communities.

We have a long, long way to go here in the U.S.—and in Lane County—before I can be comfortable referring to our current approach to incarceration as a "corrections" system.

DON'T FENCE ME OUT

I had the pleasure of spending my adolescence in a neighborhood in suburban Lancaster, Pennsylvania where I was free to roam—up and down the street to visit neighborhood kids, down the backyards to say hello to neighbors, and across the wheat field behind the house to The Woods, which was my home away from home as a child. In fact, the street I lived on was aptly named Pleasure Road.

Even if I stayed home, where I mowed the lawn, tended the flower beds, and retreated now and again to the "tree fort" in the big Norway maple tree out back, my *eyes* could still roam far and wide because there were no fences separating one yard from the next. Only our neighbors to the north, the Gerz family, had a wire, waist-high fence along the property line, but it didn't keep one's eyes from traveling beyond it.

Looking in the other direction, it was like one big park, with lawn after lawn continuing down the block, each lawn containing several large shade trees but very few shrubs to block the view. Out of respect for the neighbors—most of whom were retired—we didn't run back and forth on a regular basis from backyard to backyard, but we *could* have if we'd wanted to. And although neither kids nor adults took very frequent advantage of the "open-yard policy," we at least *saw* our neighbors on a regular basis, and if their eyes meant ours, we certainly said hello.

Few neighbors had dogs, and those who did, including my family, tied their dogs to a stake or pole when the dogs were outside in the yard, so the dogs didn't wander where they might be unwanted or get into trouble. Despite the openness of the neighborhood landscape, no one felt that they lacked privacy. It was just the way things were, and had always been. In fact, if someone had elected to erect a six-foot-high wooden fence, it would probably have been taken as an affront by the neighbors. "What did we do that they felt they had to build a fence?" Or, "What's the matter, don't they like us anymore?"

Throughout the East and the Midwest, suburban neighborhoods were largely unfenced during my youth, and most of them still are. Even here in the West, although there have always been some fences, fence mania, as I call it, doesn't appear to have taken root until the latter half of the 1900s. These days, when crossing the country from east to west, one sees very few fences until one reaches the Front Range of Colorado—Denver, Loveland, Boulder, Fort Collins. And then fences are the rule rather than the exception all the way to the Pacific.

Why is this? What is different about the West, that virtually every property in every new subdivision, from Washington to southern California, and east to Colorado, is surrounded by a six-foot wooden fence? One would think that in the formerly wide-open West, people would be *less* inclined to build fences, because there was so much space. But in fact, at least in contemporary subdivisions in the West, lot sizes are considerably smaller than lots back East, where the population is much denser. And the house and garage and driveway occupy most of the lot, so the backyard is quite tiny. But still, one has to wonder, "Why all the fences?"

If one truly feels there is a "lack of privacy" in one's backyard, there are alternatives to solid fences enclosing the yard's entire perimeter. Shrubs can be planted that will create a green screen or living fence. Or a short length of fence might be built just to shield a patio or terrace from view. But again, I recall sunbathing on the chaise longue in our backyard as a youth— in full view (if they had wanted) of the neighbors, but neither I nor they were bothered. And our family frequently had outdoor meals at the picnic table, either out back or on the big, covered front porch, again in full view of the neighbors. So what?

In my own neighborhood in Eugene now, most of which was built since the 1940s, very few yards were initially fenced. Elderly neighbors tell me of looking down the entire block of backyards on nice days and seeing yard after yard with clotheslines hung with drying clothes. Neighbors saw each other much more often, spoke with each other more, and created more of a bond than we do nowadays. Neighbors cared for each other's children, women neighbors had coffee together, and men neighbors sat on patios— no "decks" back then—and shared beers and stories.

It's not like that anymore. Weeks and even months go by when I don't see nearby neighbors. They arrive and depart by car, and when they're home, they're either inside their houses—the kids playing computer games—or they retreat to their fenced backyards to "enjoy their privacy." Unlike new subdivisions, however, there are still quite a few unfenced yards in my older neighborhood. But with every year that passes, more fences go up.

Just this fall, a neighbor on a nearby corner lot decided a fence was needed. I used to always love going by that lot, as it was so open and inviting. It did not say "keep out" as fully fenced lots do. The day the fence builders arrived, I happened to bicycle by and see the new posts already set in fresh concrete and the workers busily attending to other tasks related to the fence construction.

I stopped to say hello and to voice my regret that yet another open yard was being closed off from public view. Of course, the fence builders make a good living closing off views. The young man nonetheless acknowledged my perspective and then explained that the property's owners had recently had a number of items stolen from their yard and their new deck, so they felt they had to protect their belongings by putting up a fence.

My goodness, I explained, wouldn't it be easier and cheaper just to put one's belongings in the garage or in a backyard shed to keep them out of view when one wasn't home, or at night? And, I added, although fences provide a feeling of security to many people, they also make it much easier for thieves to operate—once the thieves have jumped the fence or gone through an unlocked gate—because the fence prevents neighbors from seeing what's going on *behind* the fence. Yes, they acknowledged, there's truth to that.

I also mentioned the option of a "discontinuous" fence that's built in part of six-foot boards, but in part of shorter boards, with a galvanized-metal grid above; or entire sections of the fence might be six-foot-high metal grid. They nodded in agreement over that idea as well.

When I went by the site again a few days later, the fence had been completed. I was pleased to see that one short section of the fence near the house was built of galvanized-metal grids instead of six-foot-high cedar boards, so from the front of the house, neighbors and passersby could in fact see into part of the backyard. Who knows? Maybe my comment a few days earlier had resulted in the small change.

Meanwhile, the fencing of the West continues, with virtually every new subdivision consuming an enormous amount of lumber in the process. And, of course, the same fences will have to be *re*-built with new lumber in another fifteen or twenty years. The best I can do for now is to set what I consider to be a good example myself. My Eugene property was already partly fenced when I moved in almost twenty years ago, but approximately half of it remains unfenced, and I plan to keep it that way.

A MESSAGE FROM JESUS

Ever since the late 1990s, when I designed and then erected a little wooden mailbox in front of my house—only a few steps from the street-side sidewalk—I occasionally find in it notes or cards from friends, visitors, or passersby. And because it's technically illegal, as I understand it, for anyone other than a bona fide U. S. Postal Service employee to place something in the box, it's always been exciting to find that someone has decided to flout authority and deposit their little message without sending it through the proper channel by placing a stamp on it.

I have occasionally found notes written by strangers to me—usually visitors who walked through my garden when I wasn't home, and wanted to ask me a question or leave a comment. The comments have always been positive, and often very touching, as people respond quite favorably to my open invitation to explore on their own the property that legally belongs to me, but that I permit anyone to visit.

Some visitors never make it past the front yard, as they begin to feel as if they're intruding on the owner's privacy—once they pass the gate into the food garden—especially if they see my bicycle leaning against the grape arbor, or spy a load of laundry flapping on the overhead line. Others feel quite comfortable poking around, and even looking in the windows to the interior of the house. I've never had this happen while I'm home, but I do now and again find the nose prints and sometimes fingerprints of those visitors on my otherwise spotlessly clean windows. And I have to smile—I'm pleased by the interest visitors have in my place, and not at all offended by what some homeowners might see as impropriety.

About a year ago, I designed and had a carpenter friend build and install a second wooden box by the cedar bench out front, where I could keep laminated information sheets about the house and garden, so visitors using the bench might be able to learn more about my property. I also have several white three-by-five cards in the glass-fronted box, as well as a pencil, and I invite comments and questions, and ask only that questioners leave an e-mail address or phone number so I might respond.

Only a few visitors so far have taken advantage of the three-by-five cards. Sometimes, it's a student of mine who stopped by in my absence and just wanted to say hello. And occasionally a visitor has some kind words of praise about his or her visit, and wishes to share those words with me.

Imagine my surprise, then, when one day I returned home from campus to find one of the three-by-five cards in my mailbox, and saw that it had been signed by *Jesus*. Wow. Was this a practical joke? Apparently not! Here, He'd stopped by my place while I was teaching that afternoon, and just wanted to let me know how much He'd enjoyed His visit:

Dear Whitey,

I think your garden is awesome because of the animals, plants, and food.

Sincerly,

Jesus

The note—with its single misspelling—was written in pencil and in what appeared to be a child's hand. Something didn't make sense. I just couldn't believe that Jesus would misspell a word, nor of course that He would visit my house in the first place. (As I've told many a friend over the years, the only thing I'm religious about is brushing my teeth.) Then it dawned on me that it wasn't GEE-zuss who'd left the note, but hay-SOOSE, the nine-year-old Latino boy who lives just three houses away with his family.

I laughed out loud right there by my mailbox!

Then I thought a bit more about my initial reaction to the note. I'd met hay-SOOSE soon after his family moved into the neighborhood a couple of years earlier, and we get along just great. I obviously know that hay-SOOSE is Spanish for GEE-zuss, but the note to me was written in English, so in my head I naturally pronounced the signer's name GEE-zuss!

Interestingly, hay-SOOSE has an older brother, Angel, whose name is AHN-hell in Spanish, but Angel pronounces it AIN-gel. I'd one time asked hay-SOOSE why AIN-gel pronounced his name the English way, but hay-SOOSE pronounces his the Spanish way. He didn't know why. But after reflecting upon it, I realized the problem that a boy named GEE-zuss would have in America. "Hey, has anyone see GEE-zuss?" "Don't mess with that bike—it belongs to GEE-zuss!" "I'm gonna ask GEE-zuss if he wants to come play soccer with us." You get the idea.

I'm just happy to call Jesus my friend—that is, hay-SOOSE my friend—and will never forget the bewildering little note he one day left for me in my mailbox.

ROSE

As I was bicycling to the grocery one afternoon, I waved to an older Asian woman I'd met before, albeit briefly. She was taking her daily walk around the neighborhood, so I stopped to say hello. We knew each other's names, but I can't say I really "knew" Rose yet.

It was October 2008, and the two-trunked coast redwood tree that stood by the sidewalk in front of my house was scheduled to be removed very soon. As Rose and I chatted curbside about the weather and about her health—remarkably good at age 84—I looked back toward my house, which was concealed from the street by the huge redwood that had branches all the way to the ground. And I asked Rose if she had noticed the sign I had put up next to the tree. She said she had not.

I explained to her that several weeks earlier, I had posted a large yellow sign beneath the tree right by the public sidewalk that informed passersby of "an important upcoming event." Here, Rose had been walking by the sign almost daily without noticing it. So, with a heavy heart, I suggested that she walk back to my place to read the sign—I couldn't bear to tell her the news myself, because I knew it would upset her. We waved goodbye, and I continued on my errand.

The next day, as I was walking out to the street, a small white envelope taped to my mailbox beneath the redwood caught my eye. The envelope said simply, "Whitey." I sat down on the nearby bench, and opened it to read:

Dear Whitey,

Please accept my heartfelt condolences on the imminent demise of your beloved coast redwood tree. We all will miss it very much. I have always enjoyed looking at and smelling that beautiful and majestic tree.

I am, a grateful neighbor,

Rose

It was a sweet and incredibly thoughtful note—and the beginning of a wonderful friendship.

Shortly thereafter, Rose invited me to drop by her house—a few blocks away and up a short hill—for "coffee." Our earlier conversations, though brief, and then the touching sympathy card, suggested to me that Rose was no ordinary octogenarian. I wanted to know more about this mysterious woman who had serendipitously come into my life. So I took her up on her offer.

I soon learned that Rose, like many older people, appreciated having some "routine" in her life. She ate a substantial breakfast right after getting up in the morning, skipped lunch, and then made herself a copious dinner. She always had orange juice with her dinner, which she'd pour into the glass well before dinnertime so it would reach room temperature by the time she drank it. And she went to bed early.

Even though she didn't eat lunch, she eagerly looked forward to her midday coffee break, when she'd make herself what she called a *latte* by heating a mugful of two-percent milk in the microwave, then stirring in two heaping teaspoons of instant coffee crystals. Along with her coffee, she always had a purchased scone from a local bakery, or a turnover from Safeway, or sometimes a cookie that her granddaughter—who lived with her—had baked.

It turned out that this was the best time of day to join Rose for a little chat, and I timed my visits accordingly. Because Rose had some difficulty with her hearing and could not hear me knock or ring her doorbell if I just stopped by, I got in the habit of telephoning her when I planned to visit. Her phone had caller identification so she always knew it was me calling. And even though she could understand little of what I said over the phone, she knew what was probably on my mind whenever I called and invariably answered, "Whitey? How are you? Can you come over for coffee?" And

I'd hop on my bike and head up the hill to her place—just a few minutes from my house.

Despite not being a coffee drinker myself, I do like warm milk *flavored* with a little coffee, and I soon joined Rose in her midday ritual—but with only a half-teaspoon of coffee crystals in the milk. Over time, Rose also learned how much I love ice cream. And because Espresso Madness ice cream from Umpqua Dairy was her usual dessert with her evening meal, she always had some in the freezer. Often, I'd add a dollop of the ice cream to my latte, or have a small bowl of it on the side—along with the usual scone, turnover, or cookie.

Initially, my visits with Rose were irregular—maybe one or two times a month—but soon the visits became an important part of my life, as well as Rose's life, and I made an effort to get over to her place at least once a week, if not twice. I looked forward to the break in my day or week, when I could just relax and talk with someone else—about nothing in particular except life itself.

Unlike my other friends, with whom I discuss mostly current events— work, play, politics, community issues—Rose was fascinated with "who I was" and how I came to be that way. She always wanted to know what was new in my life, and loved hearing about the courses I teach at the university, and my relationship with my students.

I was equally fascinated by Rose's background. Over time, I learned that she had grown up in very privileged circumstances in Shanghai, China, from the 1920s to the 1940s. Her father had attended Columbia University in New York City and, like her mother, came from a well-to-do and educated family. Rose herself was educated by English-speaking missionaries, and graduated from a Chinese university in the mid-1940s. But China's revolution forecast dramatic changes in the lives of wealthy Chinese families. Although two of her siblings remained in China and joined the revolution, Rose chose to go by ship to the U.S. in early 1947 to enroll at the University of Washington where she eventually earned a second B.A. in English Literature, and then an M.A. in Library Science.

It was at UW that she met and eventually married her husband—also a Chinese expat. And because it was still very difficult in the post-war United States for even well-educated Chinese like themselves to get jobs, they came to Eugene in 1955 and, with borrowed money, were able to buy a closed Chinese restaurant on Alder Street. Even though Rose and her husband had no experience in running a restaurant, they decided to give it a try, since nothing else looked very promising.

Within a few years, they were already doing quite well and with the help of some Eugene friends—who were also regular customers at the restaurant—they were able to purchase a nicer site at the northwest corner of 13th and Hilyard where they opened a new restaurant. It was a thriving business, but eventually, in 1980, Rose and her husband decided to sell the restaurant and retire. Her husband died several years later, and Rose never remarried.

Rose loved activity, so even after an early retirement, she found plenty to keep her busy, from volunteering at the hospital to caring for a houseful of Chinese antiques she'd collected over the years, and a yard that she maintained immaculately.

Both mentally and physically, Rose was in excellent health. Her difficulty in hearing, however, continued to worsen little by little, and despite frequent and friendly encouragement from me, she simply refused to get a hearing device. So I learned to raise my voice when we were talking—which was hard for a mostly soft-spoken guy like me, but it was the only thing I could do.

Rose and I spoke now and again about how our lives might end, and I expressed to her more than once my comfort with "taking my own life," should the need arise. She, too, thought that we should all have the option to end our lives when we no longer considered them meaningful enough to continue. All of this talk was hypothetical until summer 2014, when Rose rather suddenly began to lose interest in life—both her own as well as the lives of those around her. Although she'd always loved to read the many essays I wrote, and commented freely on them, she asked me not to bring them to her anymore. And she stopped reading the large-print versions of novels her granddaughter regularly brought home for her, at Rose's request, from the public library. More than once, she expressed to me her "listlessness" as she called it. Rose was almost 90 by then, and she had had a very good life which brought her much joy, but now her outlook had changed dramatically.

So the two of us began discussing with increasing regularity what her—or what *our*—options are when one's time appears to have come. Like most of us, she didn't wish to spend the remainder of her days as an invalid in a "rest home" where she would essentially be just warehoused until she expired. But what could she do instead? Her "affairs" were in order, and she had a Living Will that ensured that, should she have a heart attack or contract a serious illness, no extraördinary measures would be taken to prolong her life. I saw to it, too, that she completed a pink POLST (Physician Orders for Life Sustaining Treatment) form that she then excitedly taped to her refrigerator, informing emergency medical personnel that, should she collapse at home, they not attempt to resuscitate her. Now she could relax, because she had done everything possible to inform others of her desire to die, when the time came, and not have medical personnel, or her friends, or her family interfere with her wishes.

Then, on the very afternoon of her ninetieth birthday, Rose took a tumble in her kitchen and ended up in the hospital. When I visited her the next day, the first thing I said to her was, "Rose, this wasn't part of your plan." And she scowled and shook her head vigorously in agreement with my assessment. That is, following her fall—which was not life threatening— the medical establishment had no choice but to repair the damage to her hip, in an effort to help keep Rose mobile for the rest of her life instead of confined to a bed.

After she left the hospital and went to a rehabilitation center just half a block from my house, I visited her daily. She was by then increasingly distressed that she couldn't die—or wouldn't be *allowed* to die. I thought her primary goal at the time was to get well enough to return to her own home, but when I asked her point-blank what was most important to her— getting home or dying—she confirmed that it was the latter.

I inquired about getting her set up with hospice—to ensure that the end of her life would be as comfortable as possible—but because she wasn't technically "terminally ill," but just increasingly frail, hospice couldn't help. So we talked about other options for hurrying along the inevitable, and after much heartfelt discussion she elected to stop eating and drinking, except for a little water.

Although initially only she and I knew about her decision to purposefully end her own life, I urged her to share her thoughts with her family once she returned home. At the rehabilitation center, she'd been eating very, very little—just getting ready to implement her plan. Once she returned to her home, however, she stopped eating completely, and concomitantly informed her family of her decision.

The last time I saw Rose was in late October, a few days after she returned home from the rehabilitation center. Although she was physically weak and lay on the sofa in her TV room while we spoke, her mind was still sharp. Her biggest concern at that point was how long it would take until she died.

I'd been told it could be ten days to two weeks, depending on the individual. And of course Rose knew that, however long it took and whatever pain was involved, it would be a much briefer and likely less painful way to die than if she spent months or years slowly fading away in a rest home.

We had a wonderful conversation that afternoon, and I urged her in-home caregiver to be sure to take Rose into the living room every day, so she could look out the big living-room windows and see her two beloved ginkgo trees, which were just beginning to acquire their fall color. But I knew it was the last time we would talk, because Rose absolutely insisted that I not come to see her anymore as she became increasingly weak and perhaps slipped into a coma. And I respected her wish. She had both a caregiver and her granddaughter to look after her in her final days, so despite our close friendship, I didn't feel that I was abandoning her.

When I finally decided it was time for me to leave, Rose reached out her hand to hold mine—something she'd never done before—and said, "I've always admired you—*au revoir*." I would have said the very same thing to Rose, if I hadn't been so choked up about bidding her one final farewell.

Rose lived for nearly three more weeks. And almost every day, I rode my bike by her house to look at the ginkgo trees—that she and her husband had planted some fifty years before—and think about Rose who was inside turning off her light which had brightened the world for more than ninety years. The day before she died, the golden ginkgo leaves began falling, and by the next day, the two trees were almost bare. I couldn't think of a more suitable tribute to a person who thankfully shared her light with so many of us for so long.

DECEMBER THIRTY-FIRST: DAY NUMBER
THREE HUNDRED AND SIXTY-FIVE

So ends the year 2014, when I purposely declared to myself—and to anyone else who would listen—that I was staying in Lane County for the entire calendar year, just to prove a point. And what was the point? For me, it was a simple little exercise in self-restraint that helped me to focus on the wonders of my home territory, where I'd decided to settle down in 1983.

I came to Lane County because I wanted to live here. I could have gone anywhere else in the world, I suppose, but I chose this county in part because more than half of it is publicly owned land where I could wander freely and camp without being shot at for "trespassing," and in part because I'd have easy access to a variety of landscapes—"From the Coast to the Cascades," as the Lane County travel brochures say.

I now must confess, however, that I briefly left the county at three different locations during the course of the year, two of them knowingly and one inadvertently. The first two times occurred in early September during a five-day camping trip with friends to the High Cascades. As I explained in one of the preceding essays, our group first visited Lane County's southeast corner where, simply for convenience, we briefly strayed into Douglas County in order to get as close as possible to the corner by road. Had I been alone, I would have gone overland through a half-mile or so of forest to reach the corner; but I didn't think I should drag my friends through that unfamiliar and trail-less stretch of woods with me, just to make a point.

As I explained in another essay, I chose to make a similar detour only a few days later when the same group of friends and I visited Lane County's *northeast* corner near McKenzie Pass, and we strayed briefly into Linn County. Again, I could have walked over a half-mile of extremely rough lava myself—in order to make a point—but because I was with a group of good-natured friends that I wanted to *keep* as my friends, I chose not to force them to walk across the lava bed with me.

The third place I sneaked by the nonexistent Lane County border police was simply a mistake on my part. To scout out a field trip to the Cascades that I would be leading in May for my University of Oregon students, I took the McKenzie Bridge bus upriver, along with my bike, and then bicycled from the McKenzie River Ranger Station to Olallie Creek Road, where I wanted to show the class a particularly interesting site. For some reason, I'd thought the line between Lane and Linn counties crossed Highway 126 near Clear Lake—several miles north of Olallie Creek Road. But it wasn't until I was on my way back down 126 later in the afternoon that I passed the sign saying, "Welcome to Lane County" and did a double take. I thought the sign had been misplaced, so certain was I that I had not left Lane County. But upon my return to Eugene and after a look at a good topographic map, I had to regretfully acknowledge my error. Oops.

I actually trespassed into Linn County two *more* times the following weekend, when I took half of my large class to visit the Olallie Creek Road site on Saturday, and half on Sunday. On neither day did any of the students—who were aware of my goal of staying within Lane County for the year—notice the roadside county-line sign, or at least nobody said anything to me about it. And I kept quiet about it myself, until now, simply out of embarrassment at having made the mistake.

My year in Lane County has been notable, both for what activities I *did* engage in, as well as for those I did *not*. For example, I spent a *lot* of days outside, including 73 days alone in "the woods" near McKenzie Bridge. I taught five one-day field trips: two in the West Cascades for my aforementioned Trees Across Oregon course at the University of Oregon, and three for my OUT-OF-DOORS business (one at Tire Mountain near Westfir; one in the Bryce Creek and Holland Meadows area southwest of Oakridge; and one in the Coast Range near Triangle Lake). And I went on two camping trips with other people: three days to the coast with a friend to celebrate my birthday, and five days in the High Cascades with a group of friends. That makes a total of 86 days in the "wilds" of Lane County—nearly a quarter of the year. I also spent 28 nights in my tent, all but two of those in the Cascades.

A couple of other noteworthy things I did in 2014 include bicycling some 3,000 miles—mostly within the urban growth boundary of Eugene. And I cared for a productive home garden which provided almost all of the fruits and vegetables I consumed during the course of the year, except for a few wintertime trips to the produce department of a local grocery to buy Brussels sprouts and bananas, both of which I like and neither of which I grow.

But what did this overeducated, politically and socially liberal, food-loving, tree-hugging, and financially comfortable Lane County resident *not* do in 2014 that might be expected of his ilk?

- I did not attend the Oregon Country Fair.
- I never once listened to National Public Radio nor watched Oregon Public Broadcasting on television. (I don't even own a radio or a television.)
- I didn't buy a single cup of coffee.
- I did not purchase, wear, or gaze admiringly upon any piece of tie-dyed clothing.
- I attended no concerts, indoors or out.
- I ate in restaurants only two times, both of which were at the invitation of friends. (However, I did eat "out"—that is, out-of-doors—for about a quarter of my nearly 1,100 meals during the year.)
- I rode in a privately owned vehicle driven by someone else only five times; and coincidentally, I drove one myself only five times.
- I never once made a disparaging remark about a "clearcut." (Technically, clearcuts are illegal in Oregon, and even *apparent* clearcuts upset me no more than a just-cut field of wheat.)

I did, however, hug a few trees—including one of the largest and oldest London plane-trees in Oregon, just before University of Oregon contractors cut it down to make room for a new building on campus.

In other words, I'm a "typical Lane County resident" only in the sense that I am unique—like everyone else. And my habits and activities cannot be predicted, based solely on the socioeconomic stratum of which I am a part.

During the course of the year 2014, I realized, too, that I'd incidentally achieved a milestone in my life here in Lane County: I reached the point where I can now say that I've spent *most* of my life here. I arrived in Eugene on the last day of June in 1983, and nine days later celebrated my first birthday in Lane County and my thirty-first on the planet. And in July of 2014, I celebrated my *thirty-second* birthday in Lane County, and my *sixty-second* on the planet. So I've now spent slightly more than half of my life here.

Like many other Lane County residents, I came here from "away," having been born and raised in Pennsylvania, worked abroad for several years, and attended graduate school first in Corvallis, Oregon and then in Madison, Wisconsin. Although Lane County may not—for whatever reasons—turn out to be paradise for every immigrant, I'm mighty glad to have found my own little piece of heaven-on-earth here, right between the coast and the Cascades.